KENYA

THE BEAUTIFUL

KENYA

THE BEAUTIFUL

NH

NEW HOLLAND

First published in 1995 by
New Holland (Publishers) Ltd
London • Cape Town • Sydney

ISBN 1 85368 557 7

New Holland (Publishers) Ltd
24 Nutford Place, London W1H 6DQ

Managing editor Mariëlle Renssen
Editor Christine Riley
Design and DTP Darren MacGurk
Proofreader Tessa Kennedy
Cartographer Darren McLean

Reproduction by Hirt & Carter (Pty) Ltd, Cape Town
Printed and bound in Singapore by Tien Wah Press (Pte) Ltd

PHOTOGRAPHIC CREDITS
Daryl and Sharna Balfour: pages 89, 160, 161 • **Daryl and Sharna
Balfour/SIL:** pages 5, 6, 11, 12, 18 below, 19, 22, 31, 34, 35, 36, 37, 40 above, 50
above & below, 51, 52, 54/55, 58, 59, 62, 74, 75, 76, 80, 82, 84 above, 86 below,
92, 93, 94, 95, 100, 101 top, above & right, 102, 103, 104, 105 top & above, 106,
115, 116 above & below, 117, 120, 121, 124, 125, 128 above & below, 129, 130,
131 above & below, 132 below, 142, 144 left & right, 146, 147 left & right, 148
below, 150, 151 above & below, 159 • **Daryl and Sharna Balfour/ABPL:** page 82
• **Andrew Bannister/SIL:** cover, pages 23 below, 33 above right, 28, 30, 38, 39
below, 44, 45, 48, 49, 57, 61 above, 65, 68, 69 above, 70, 71 left & right, 72, 73
above, 77 above, 88 above, 99, 108 above & below, 109, 110, 111, 114, 132 above,
136 above & below, 137, 138, 139, 140, 153 above, 154 • **Anthony
Bannister/ABPL:** page 85 • **Peter Blackwell:** pages 10, 20, 83, 84 below,
86 above, 87, 88 below, 90 above & below, 98 above, 165 • **Colin Bell:** page 17 •
Alan Binks: pages 16 above, 29 above, 63, 66, 79, 113, 127, 134 • **Michael
Brett:** pages 15, 23 above, 46, 53 above, 56, 60, 61 below, 73 below, 98 below,
145, 166 right • **Camerapix:** page 18 above • **Gerald Cubitt:** page 97, 156 •
Roger de la Harpe: page 164 above • **Pat Evans:** page 21 below • **Kerstin
Geier/ABPL:** page 143 • **Dirk Heinrich:** page 21 above • **I Lichtenberg/Photo
Access:** 12 below, 25, 32, 33 below, 118/119 • **Jeannie Mackinnon:** pages 26,
112 right & left, 126 middle & below • **Alain Proust/Fair Lady Magazine:** pages
12 above, 16 below, 39 above, 40 below, 41, 42, 43, 53 below, 64, 122 above &
below, 123 • **Mitch Reardon:** pages 1, 2/3 • **Dave Richards:** pages 14, 29 below,
33 above left, 69 below, 77, 78 left & right, 96, 133, 158, 161, 162, 163 above &
below • **Anup Shah/ABPL:** pages 91, 149, 155 • **David Steele/Photo Access:**
pages 28, 141, 148 above • **Bruce Trzebinski:** pages 126 top, 156 •
Clive Ward: pages 152, 153 below, 168.

[ABPL: Anthony Bannister Photo Library • SIL: Struik Image Library]

Acknowledgements: The author wishes to thank Dr David Western,
director of the Kenya Wildlife Service, and Wilbur Ottichilo, head of the
research division, for their enthusiastic assistance.

CONTENTS

THE LIE OF THE LAND

*I*N KENYA'S DISTANT PAST, powerful forces deep within the earth's molten centre rose to the surface tearing a long rent in the crust. Fiery streams of lava flowed out of the cracks blanketing a vast area in molten rock, while volcanoes spewed fire and ash into the atmosphere. Along this line of weakness, subsequent periods of violent faulting occurred. The floor of the long valley sank, displacing molten rock upwards along its sides. In the deep floor of the valley, lakes formed in depressions, and one by one the volcanoes ceased spouting and fell silent.

The Rift Valley that passes through Kenya on its 6 000-kilometre journey from Israel to Mozambique is one of the most impressive volcanic regions in the world. Within the borders of Kenya the Rift Valley achieves one of its most dramatic expressions, and 11 dormant volcanoes puncture the valley floor. In some places boiling springs bring soda to the surface turning the water bitter in many of the Rift Valley lakes. Africa's second highest mountain, Mount Kenya, towering to 5 199 metres on the central highlands, is an ancient volcano that has been weathered by wind and ice. Although once tumultuous and destructive, the geological forces that produced the Rift Valley fault and the immense volcanic outpourings brought about the fertile soils that today make Kenya's cash-crop exports of tea, coffee and tobacco possible.

The country can easily be divided into three areas: the fertile Rift Valley highlands, the savanna lowlands to the east and south, and the deserts of the north.

The Rift Valley highlands, squeezed and stretched into high plateaus and deep valleys, are home to the overwhelming majority of Kenya's people. The highlands' agreeable equatorial climate, productive soils weathered from volcanic outpourings rich in minerals, and reliable rainfall, have been well utilized and now produce Kenya's cash crops of coffee, tea, tobacco and pyrethrum. On these highlands, five mountain ranges exceed 3 000 metres in height. The Cheranganis plunge 1 700 metres in five kilometres down the Elgeyo Escarpment to the thorn-covered Kerio Valley. Flanked by the lofty forested peaks of the Mau Escarpment and the Aberdares, the Rift Valley cuts through the centre of the region, carving the high-altitude lakes of Nakuru, Elmenteita and Naivasha. Winds blowing inland from the Indian Ocean are trapped by these high mountains giving rise to the Tana, Athi and Ewaso Nyiro rivers. To the west of these temperate highlands, the extensive inland sea of Lake Victoria – almost the area of Scotland – gathers the waters that empower the Nile on its 6 670-kilometre journey to the Mediterranean.

The fertile highlands are a geographical anomaly in Kenya. Nearly two-thirds of Kenya is a bush-covered lowland inhabited by small bands of nomads who herd cattle, goats and camels across sun-scorched savannas in search of grazing. In this region, rainfall is erratic and meagre, except where high volcanic mountains catch moisture from the surrounding desert and convert it to forest, or where oceanic winds water a narrow coastal strip. In the far north of this region, a 6 400-square-kilometre jade-coloured lake seems out of place in the searing wilderness. Lake Turkana is the largest desert lake in the world, and with no outlet to the sea, the lake's mineral-rich waters taste like canned soda water.

Cover: A feathered fantasy – flamingos backlit on Lake Bogoria.

Page 1: A hunter-gatherer of the Ndorobo tribe.

Pages 2/3: Lionesses in the Masai Mara National Reserve.

Page 5: Elephant in the Amboseli National Park.

Page 6: Dhows off Shanzu Beach on the north coast of Kenya.

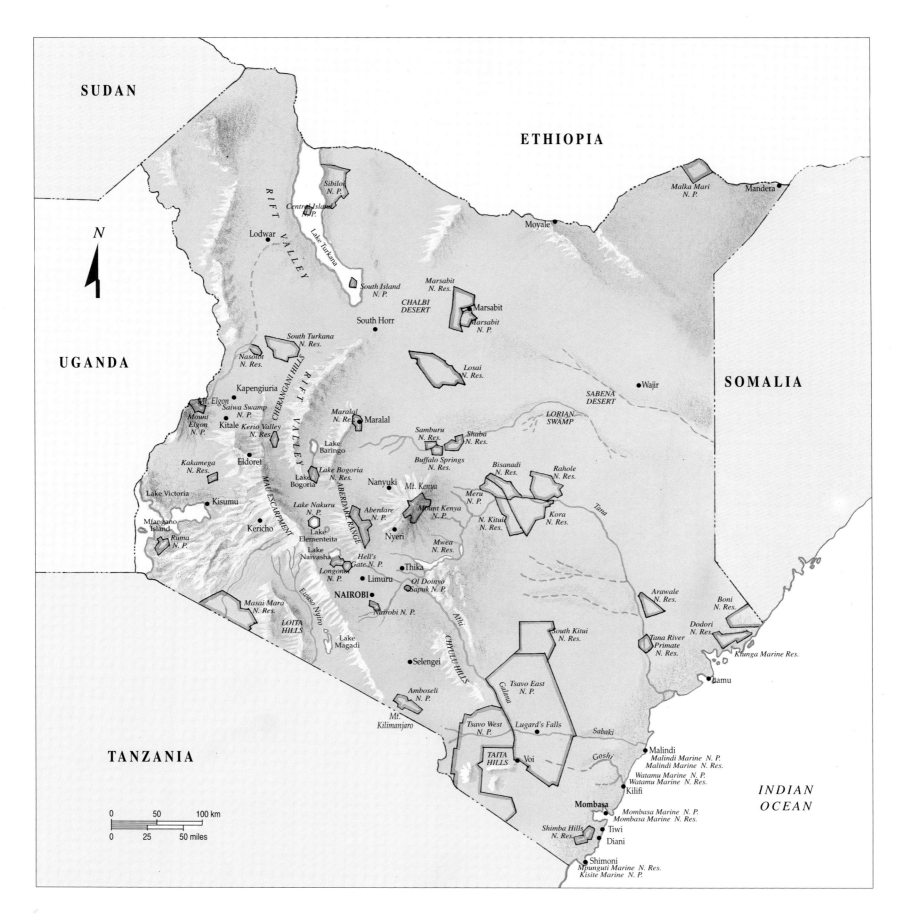

SUDAN

ETHIOPIA

UGANDA

SOMALIA

TANZANIA

INDIAN OCEAN

Sibiloi N. P.

Central Island N. P.

Malka Mari N. P.

Mandera

Lodwar

Moyale

Lake Turkana

South Island N. P.

Marsabit

Marsabit N. Res.

CHALBI DESERT

South Horr

Marsabit N. P.

South Turkana N. Res.

Nasolot N. Res.

Losai N. Res.

Wajir

Kapengiuria

SABENA DESERT

Mt. Elgon

Saiwa Swamp N. P.

Maralal N. Res.

Maralal

LORIAN SWAMP

Mount Elgon N. P.

Kitale

Kerio Valley N. Res.

Samburu N. Res.

Shaba N. Res.

Lake Baringo

Kakamega N. Res.

Eldoret

Buffalo Springs N. Res.

Bisanadi N. Res.

Rahole N. Res.

Lake Bogoria

Lake Bogoria N. Res.

Nanyuki

Mt. Kenya

Lake Victoria

Kisumu

Lake Nakuru N. P.

Meru N. P.

Kora N. Res.

Tana

Mfangano Island

Kericho

Aberdare N. P.

Mount Kenya N. P.

Ruma N. P.

Lake Elementeita

Nyeri

N. Kitui N. Res.

Mwea N. Res.

Lake Naivasha

Hell's Gate N. P.

Thika

Longonot N. P.

Limuru

Ol Doinyo Sapuk N. P.

NAIROBI

Arawale N. Res.

Boni N. Res.

Masai Mara N. Res.

Nairobi N. P.

Dodori N. Res.

LOITA HILLS

Lake Magadi

South Kitui N. Res.

Tana River Primate N. Res.

Kiunga Marine Res.

Selengei

Lamu

Amboseli N. P.

Tsavo East N. P.

Mt. Kilimanjaro

Tsavo West N. P.

Lugard's Falls

Sabaki

Malindi

Malindi Marine N. P.
Malindi Marine N. Res.

TAITA HILLS

Voi

Goshi

Watamu Marine N. P.
Watamu Marine N. Res.

Kilifi

Mombasa

Mombasa Marine N. P.
Mombasa Marine N. Res.

Shimba Hills N. Res.

Tiwi

Diani

Shimoni

Mpunguti Marine N. Res.
Kisite Marine N. P.

RIFT VALLEY

CHERANGANI HILLS

MAU ESCARPMENT

ABERDARE RANGE

CHYULU HILLS

Ewaso Ngiro

Athi

Galana

0   50   100 km

0   25   50 miles

N

9

INTRODUCTION

Cheetah (left) frequent the grasslands of the Masai Mara National Reserve, where they can be easily observed by tourists. Cheetah are nervous animals and may even be chased off their kills by flocks of vultures. After killing their prey, cheetah eat very rapidly to minimize detection by scavengers and other predators.

The Uhuru Monument (below) lies south of Nairobi's central business district, on Langata Road and adjacent to Wilson Airport. It commemorates Kenya's first 20 years of independence. A white dove of peace, and two hands clasped together in unity, form the monument's central piece. Kenya attained independence on 12 December 1963 after nearly 70 years of colonial administration.

Kenya accounts for less than two per cent of Africa's 30.3-million square-kilometre landmass. Yet every year, some 800 000 tourists from Europe and North America are drawn to a land rich in human history, culture, scenic grandeur and, in the closing years of the twentieth century, a land that still contains spacious wildlands little influenced by the march of progress. On the extensive prairies and in the forests of North America, 11 species of deer and antelope can be found. In Africa, 77 antelope species occur, half of which may be seen in Kenya. This proliferation of antelope, supplemented by herds of zebra, giraffe, wild pig, rhino, elephant and a dozen primates, supports the predators for which Kenya's savannas are world renowned: lion, leopard, cheetah, hyena, wild dog and jackal. Apart from the mammals, 1 035 of the world's 9 000 bird species occur in Kenya.

Jomo Kenyatta International Airport in Nairobi is most visitors' first destination in Kenya. From the busy arrival hall of the airport, situated 16 kilometres southeast of central Nairobi, a six-lane highway crosses the corn-coloured grasslands of the Athi Plains. Having joined the Nairobi to Mombasa road, the route heads towards the distinctive skyline of Nairobi's business district. While the symbols of modern urbanity are everywhere apparent, a Masai giraffe may be spotted feeding on an acacia bush at the roadside. Only a few years ago, the airport highway had to be closed after lions had occupied the road.

At first sight, Nairobi is an impressive city. The airport road carries the visitor down tree-lined Uhuru Avenue's wide carriageway. To the left, Uhuru Park cuts a green swathe between the city centre and the suburbs to the west. To the right, along Uhuru Avenue, imposing buildings erected since independence hint at the concentration of economic power in the city. However, even by African standards the central business district of Nairobi is small. Bounded by Uhuru Highway to the west, the railway and station to the south, and Nairobi River to the northeast, Kenya's economic and political centre covers an area of less than four square kilometres. However, central Nairobi's compactness can be deceiving – the city's extensive suburbs cover 500 square kilometres and are now home to nearly two million people.

Nairobi has its origins in the decisions of a railway engineer. In 1896 British colonial interests in East Africa centred on the construction of a railway from Mombasa to Uganda. It took six years to construct the railway from the coast to Lake Victoria. The cost of laying 1 000 kilometres of track was estimated at £3.6 million which was an excessive amount of money at the time. In fact, the final costs totalled a staggering £7.9 million. Within the British parliament, opposition members denounced the railway project, and it was not long before it became christened 'The Lunatic Line'.

Some 30 000 Indian labourers were shipped from Bombay to Mombasa and construction of the railway went ahead, but not without incident. At the bridge over the Tsavo River – now within Kenya's largest national park – two man-eating lions killed 28 workmen before being destroyed by one Colonel Patterson, who had been ordered to Tsavo in 1898 to take charge of the construction of the bridge. His adventures are recalled in *The Man-Eaters of Tsavo*.

After ascending from the coastal plain and the impenetrable scrub thickets of Tsavo, the railway followed a direct route across the open Athi Plains. To the north, the country was hilly and inhabited by Kikuyu farmers; to the south, the parched savannas of Maasailand lacked permanent watering points. The Nairobi River offered the most southerly supply of permanent water, and so the engineers plotted a route that attempted to take these factors into account. Thus it was that the railway reached Mile 327 and the valley known to Maasai herders as *Ewaso Nyrobi*, or 'stream of cold water', on 30 May 1899. Ahead lay a daunting task. The Ngong Hills, immortalized in Karen Blixen's *Out of Africa*, formed the eastern wall of the Great Rift Valley behind the railhead. It was in this area too that the dense rainforests of the highlands, now partly replaced by suburbs and smallholdings, began. In a country inhabited by man-eating lions and covered in uncharted thicket and savanna, the railway represented the only practical means of transport into the interior. People immediately began to pour into the settlement. A disorderly assortment of tents and temporary wood-and-iron bungalows soon resulted, and the first makeshift shops were erected along the muddy tracks that were mapped out on the plain.

At the height of construction 22 000 workmen were employed on the railway. The temporary headquarters soon became permanent, and infant Nairobi rapidly developed into an overcrowded, squalid camp with an inadequate water supply. The settlement bordered on a swamp that, combined with the waterlogged clay soils of the site, created ideal conditions for malaria-carrying mosquitoes. Within the first year, more than 700 residents died, many of them from malaria. Despite its poor location, Nairobi continued to expand at a rapid pace. When Sir Winston Churchill visited it in 1907 he remarked that it was already too late to relocate the town to a better site.

Much has changed since Churchill's visit. For centuries the ancient coastal cities had been the focal points of trade, and the British colonial government was housed in Mombasa. Today, from a combination of economic development and resultant population growth, the core area of Kenya has shifted to the central highlands and the shores of Lake Victoria. In these two regions 75 per cent of Kenya's 29 million people now live on one-tenth of the land. Given its location relative to the most developed regions of Kenya, and situated at the junction of all major transport routes, it is not surprising that Nairobi has become East Africa's principal city.

In Nairobi's street names and in many of its buildings, reminders of Kenya's political history can be found. West of Uhuru Park on Nairobi Hill, the colony's seven-member and all-white legislative council held its first session in 1907. A visit to parliament, in the city centre, is a reminder of the city's long involvement with the country's constitutional development. Across the road from parliament, the grassed expanse of City Square – encircled by the Kenyatta Conference Centre, the Law Courts and the City Hall – is an ideal place to begin an exploration of the city.

The Kenyatta International Conference Centre seats 4 000 delegates and regularly hosts international conferences. From the restaurant on the 28th floor, it is possible to see the peaks of Kilimanjaro and Mount Kenya on a clear day. On the northern edge of the city centre, Harry Thuku Road, separating the university and the Norfolk Hotel, recalls the 1922 arrest of Harry Thuku, leader of the first black political movement. It was near the hotel that police fired on a crowd protesting the arrest of Thuku, killing 25 people.

A large statue of Kenya's first president, Jomo Kenyatta, occupies the promenade between the conference centre and the Law Courts. Born near Nairobi, Kenyatta took his first job as a water-meter inspector for the Nairobi municipality. After spending 15 years abroad, mostly in Britain, he returned to Kenya in 1946. As the leader of the Kenya Africa Union (KAU) – a moderate black political movement – he was arrested in 1952 and detained for nine years for alleged Mau Mau involvement. Although Kenyatta denied the charge, he served as a convenient scapegoat to the colonial authorities. Ironically, if Kenyatta had not been detained, it appears likely that he would have been the object of an assassination attempt by radical factions within the Mau Mau. In 1961, with many of the Mau Mau guerrillas still in detention, the authorities consented to release Kenyatta, two years prior to the granting of independence. The *Mzee*, or 'wise old man', occupied a centrist position in Kenyan politics throughout his life, and maintained close ties with Britain during the 15 years he served as president. Following Kenyatta's death in 1978, vice president Daniel arap Moi was chosen as president. One of Nairobi's two main thoroughfares is named in his honour.

Despite the tumultuous events of the past, Nairobi is today as vibrant and friendly as any of the world's major cities. For many tourists, the tudor-styled Norfolk Hotel, situated across the road from the university, and the New Stanley Hotel's Thorn Tree Café, surrounding an enormous yellow-fever tree, are both favourite rendezvous points. From either venue, the city's

The Lunatic Line (above) reached the banks of the Tsavo River in 1898. The construction of the railway bridge over the river was brought to a halt by two man-eating lions who ultimately succeeded in devouring 28 Indian labourers who had been recruited in Bombay to complete the project. Colonel Patterson was ordered to the site to take charge of the construction of the bridge, but he was forced to spend much of his time in pursuit of the lions. Ten months would pass before Patterson finally succeeded in destroying the man-eaters.

Self-employed Kenyans produce a variety of products ranging from hand-carved curios and wooden chairs (above) to steel implements. These roadside entrepreneurs, referred to as the *Jua-kali*, meaning 'hot sun' (they often work outdoors), are a common sight in any town or city in Kenya. Unemployment remains a serious concern. The *Jua-kali*, or informal sector, therefore provides valuable employment opportunities that are often lacking in the formal economy.

The Giraffe Centre (above) has an impressive manor and attractive gardens that evoke images of Woburn Abbey and similar English safari parks. The giraffe belong to the Rothschild's subspecies, restricted in number to about 500 animals.

many curio shops, bookshops, restaurants, art galleries, museums, markets and various buildings are easily accessible. Apart from these two establishments, Nairobi has a wide range of hotels and other forms of accommodation that offer anything from country-style accommodation within the city centre to the five-star luxury and exclusivity of the Nairobi Hilton. Nairobi's taxi-drivers are legendary for their inventive driving skills. On every corner of the city, eager taxi-drivers driving anything from authentic London cabs to dilapidated saloon cars compete for the visitor's attention. Thanks to an abundance of *matatus*, or taxis (there are over 100 000 in Kenya), getting from one location in Nairobi to another is as quick and trouble-free as it would be in any city in Europe.

Upper Nairobi's suburbs, such as Muthaiga and Westlands, offer convenient shopping and comfortable living. Muthaiga is the city's most exclusive suburb. Once used for dairy farming, the fertile soil of Muthaiga has been divided into the manicured, tree-filled gardens of Nairobi's millionaires and ambassadors. The pink façade of the exclusive Muthaiga Club – where Karen Blixen and Denys Finch Hatton met in 1918 – is perhaps Kenya's last grand monument to the colonial past.

Ten kilometres further west, past the Ngong Road Forest, which is still home to leopards and monkeys, the suburbs of Langata and Karen provide an almost sylvan existence. Over half of Kenya's 50 000 whites live in Nairobi, most of them in these suburbs. The grand homes, fashioned from quarried stone set in gardens carved out of the forest, are reminiscent of the affluent suburbs of North America. However, in a city of nearly two million inhabitants, many of them unemployed, robberies and violent crimes are on the increase. High walls, security fences and security guards are features as characteristic of the affluent suburbs as their tall trees and spacious gardens.

A visit to Karen Blixen's house at the foot of the Ngong Hills is highly recommended. In 1917 Karen Blixen endeavoured to grow coffee on the surrounding land. Fourteen years later, with a failed coffee crop and the family finances exhausted, she was forced to leave the farm, and Africa, and sail back to Denmark. Although the suburb of Karen has spread over the former coffee lands, the house, with its spacious garden and views of the picturesque Ngong Hills still inhabited by buffalo, evokes images of the colonial past. Many of Nairobi's suburbs are not quite as picturesque. The northern suburb of Parklands, which was once an Indian precinct, is today showing visible signs of decay. Eastleigh and the eastern suburbs such as Kimathi and Dandora, swollen by immigrants to the city, have become home to middle-income earners. To the northeast of central Nairobi, thousands scrape out an existence in the dire slum of Mathare Valley, and even within walking distance of the city centre itself, densely packed shanty towns have taken root on scraps of land. Some of the shanty dwellers have found employment in Kenya's booming informal sector. They can be seen forging steel items at sidewalk foundries, nurturing plants in small-scale nurseries, or hawking curios to the ever-increasing tourist trade. At suburban intersections, makeshift stalls sell goods such as fruit and take-aways.

Wild Kenya begins only five kilometres south of parliament. Proclaimed in 1946, Nairobi National Park holds the distinction of being the first national park established in Kenya. Although the 117-square-kilometre area of savanna and forest is small compared to most African parks, close proximity to Nairobi and the sheer diversity of wildlife and habitats conserved within its boundaries, guarantee popularity. In 1993 as many as 164 565 people visited the park, exceeding the number of visitors to the ever-popular Masai Mara National Reserve.

It is almost incomprehensible that a tourist sitting at the Thorn Tree Café, adjacent to Kenyatta Avenue's crowded lanes of traffic, could be photographing lion or cheetah at a kill in less than 30 minutes. Apart from the sizable lion and cheetah population, leopard, hyena and jackal still frequent the park. Buffalo herds roam across the grasslands with Nairobi's skyline as the backdrop, while hippo and crocodile occur in pools in the Athi River. From an elevated lookout near the main entrance, the open savanna stretches uninterrupted to a distant range of mauve hills. Twelve species of antelope, including kongoni, wildebeest, impala, gazelle and eland, are common and gather seasonally in large herds on the open grassland that clothes the eastern three-quarters of the park.

While it has been necessary to erect fences on three sides of the park, the southern boundary is unfenced and the adjoining Kitengela Corridor still permits migratory herds of game from southern Maasailand to enter the park. Given its location, and an abundance both in diversity and quantity of game, it could be mistaken for a safari park or a contrived tourist trap. It is neither. Nairobi National Park is an entirely natural system and, apart from black rhino translocated from elsewhere in Kenya, the animals present are all descendants of those that roamed the plains on the day the first railway worker arrived.

The attractive headquarters of the Kenya Wildlife Service, headed by Dr David Western, are located next to the main entrance to the park. Restructured in 1989 after a drastic rise in elephant poaching, this semi-autonomous body is responsible for managing Kenya's 25 000 square kilometres of national parks and 15 000 square kilometres of national reserves. Across the road, the Animal Orphanage is the closest thing in Kenya to a zoo. Nearby, Daphne Sheldrick, of the David Sheldrick Conservation Foundation, raises orphaned black rhinos and elephants.

The black-and-white colobus monkey (above) is common in the moist forests of the Aberdares, Mount Kenya and western Kenya. In the past colobus monkeys were heavily hunted for their fine pelts, but are now strictly protected. They spend much of the day high in the forest canopy. Extremely agile monkeys, they are often seen leaping from tree to tree, with their tails flowing out behind them.

North of Nairobi, the fertile smallholdings of the Central Province divide the land between the prominent peaks of Mount Kenya and the Aberdares into a patchwork of coffee fields, tea plantations and dairy farms. After the completion of the Uganda Railway, Maasai grazing land to the north of the railway was reserved solely for English settlers. Land that had served as a buffer between rival tribes was further utilized for the same purpose, and an area of 31 000 square kilometres was reserved for white settlers. Thus the land on the road to Thika and the land north of Nyeri became part of the 'white highlands'.

After independence some two-thirds of the white-owned farms were expropriated in a scheme financed by the British government, and the land was allocated to 34 000 families. Due to the fertile soils and the potential for cash crops, population densities in the Central Province are second only to those of the margins of Lake Victoria. In places, the population exceeds 400 people per square kilometre. The protected forests of the high Aberdares and Mount Kenya are therefore in sharp contrast to the intensively cultivated farms of the lower slopes. Smallholders on the central highlands produce 60 per cent of Kenya's fine arabica coffee. Introduced by missionaries in 1901, coffee has become a principal earner of foreign exchange. The smallholders also produce over half of Kenya's tea.

The luxuriant forest that envelops the backbone of the Aberdares (known by the Kikuyu as *Nyandarua*, or 'drying hide') provided refuge for several thousand guerrillas during the Mau Mau rebellion. Of all Africa's conflicts and independence struggles, the Mau Mau episode is one that is largely surrounded by myth and misinterpretation. The Mau Mau uprising had its origins in World War I and the discriminatory treatment of returning black soldiers. In the 1920s, after strong pressure from London, the settlers allowed Indians and Arabs six of the 17 seats on the legislative council. It was only in 1944 that the first black Kenyan (Eliud Mathu) was nominated to the council.

During World War II many black Kenyans fought once again for Britain. After the war, in response to increasing settler domination of the best land and all aspects of political life, militant opposition to the status quo began to emerge. The Mau Mau movement, essentially a peasant revolt, soon enjoyed widespread support. In 1952 a state of emergency was declared. Mau Mau fighters fled to the highland forests, and 50 000 British troops were sent to Kenya. While it has often been portrayed as a bitter struggle against white farmers on the highlands, only 32 white civilians and about 50 British soldiers were killed. African casualties, on the other hand, totalled 11 000 Mau Mau fighters and 2 000 civilians. Four years of conflict had cost the British taxpayer £60 million, and enthusiasm for supporting an exclusive white settler system began to diminish. Policy changes followed and by 1960 black Kenyans were allowed to purchase farmland, although many of the forest fighters remained in hiding until independence.

In the lush fields and valleys of the highlands, all signs of the conflict have long been obscured. Today, the dark massif of the Aberdares provides refuge to an abundance of forest animals. The lofty 1 800 square kilometres of national park and adjoining forest reserve still contain an estimated 2 800 elephant as well as numerous buffalo, leopard, lion, waterbuck, bushbuck, bushpig and a few black rhino.

Vegetation in the Aberdares is largely affected by altitude. Dense montane rainforests cover the lower slopes up to around the 2 400-metre mark, bamboo thickets clothe the slopes up to about 3 000 metres, moss-wrapped hagenia forest occurs up to 3 400 metres, and above this zone the open moors stretch to the high peaks. From the town of Nyeri a track climbs through bamboo thickets and twisted, lichen-festooned hagenia forest to the misty moors, icy rivers and spectacular waterfalls of the lofty Aberdares. Ol Doinyo Lesatima, at 3 999 metres, is the highest peak in the Aberdares. The route passes the impressive Gura, Kurura and Chania falls, Kenya's highest and most dramatic waterfalls.

The Aberdares are world famous for two forest game lodges, Treetops and The Ark. The lodges combine comfort and close-up game-viewing in idyllic forest settings. The oldest of the forest lodges, Treetops began as a simple tree house built in 1932. Enlarged over the years in response to growing popularity, the lodge was burned down in 1954 by the Mau Mau fighters and rebuilt a few years later. Located deeper in the forest, at an altitude of 2 300 metres, The Ark is the highest game lodge in Kenya. A third, the three-storey Mountain Lodge, is located on the western slopes of Mount Kenya. Hidden in a dense forest, it is the only forest lodge accessible by private car. Unusual forest animals, such as the elusive chestnut-coloured bongo, the giant forest hog, Sykes' monkey and the exquisite black-and-white colobus monkey, are attracted to the lodges by the water and mud wallows. As the ambience and game-viewing possibilities are unique in Africa, it is not surprising that many tourist itineraries include a night at one of these lodges.

Tourists visiting the Aberdare lodges first meet either at the Aberdare Country Club, or the impressive Outspan Hotel in Nyeri, where Lord Baden-Powell, founder of the World Scout Movement, is buried. North of Nyeri, on the dry savannas of the Laikipia district, wildlife is plentiful. While cattle farming is the predominant pursuit on the vast commercial ranches of the district, on several ranches, such as Solio, Lewa Downs, Ol Pejeta and Ol Jogi, sanctuaries have been created for Kenya's greatly reduced black rhino, and for white rhino imported from the Hluhluwe-Umfolozi Park in South Africa.

*T*hirty kilometres east of the Aberdares, across an open plain, Mount Kenya ascends to meet the ceiling of cloud that obscures the peaks from view for most of the day. Mount Kenya's profile is typically that of an isolated volcano. From a base measuring roughly 60 kilometres across, the mountain rises steeply towards the summit. The upper reaches, above 4 000 metres, measure from 10 to 17 kilometres across. Centuries before the first European explorers ventured into the interior of Kenya, the Wakamba people of the low-lying plains to the east believed that the dark peaks and white glaciers floating above the clouds resembled the black-and-white plumage of a male ostrich. *Kiinya*, a Wakamba word meaning 'the hill of the ostrich', is the most likely origin of the name 'Kenya'. Mount Kenya has played a significant role in both the traditional and religious life of the people of the central highlands. The Kikuyu believed the mountain brought rain, and in times of drought prayers would be offered to Ngai, the god who dwells in the high peaks. The Kikuyu call the mountain *Kere Nyaga* or *Kirinyaga*, meaning 'white mountain' or 'place of brightness'. Apart from being the throne of Ngai, for the Kikuyu the mountain has further significance. According to Kikuyu legend, Ngai took Gikuyu, the first Kikuyu, to the top of the mountain and showed him the beauty of the land that he had given him. Descending from the mountain, Gikuyu found that Ngai had provided him with a wife, Mumbi. The couple built a house and raised nine daughters who, after Ngai had provided them with husbands, became the forebears of the nine Kikuyu clans.

The first European explorer to encounter the mountain was the German missionary, Ludwig Krapf, in 1849. Krapf reported seeing 'two large horns or pillars covered with a white substance' from Kitui, about 160 kilometres to the east. Krapf had to wait 34 years before his story was confirmed by the Scottish traveller, Joseph Thomson, who, from the nearby Aberdare range, saw 'a gleaming snow-white peak with sparkling facets'. It was not until 1899, and after three abortive attempts, that Halford Mackinder succeeded in climbing Batian. The lower peak, Nelion, was only climbed for the first time in 1929 by Wyn Harris and Eric Shipton, the latter subsequently becoming one of Britain's best Himalayan climbers. While the Kikuyu are thought to have climbed the mountain prior to Mackinder's attempts, the first documented ascent by a Kenyan was completed in 1959 by Kisoi Munyao.

Although the surrounding highlands are somewhat densely populated, there is a 717-square-kilometre national park protecting the mountain's upper reaches, a contiguous 2 000-square-kilometre forest reserve safeguarding the lower. Together, they protect one of the most important relics of Afro-montane vegetation in Africa. In 1978 the national park as well as much of the forest reserve were granted Biosphere Reserve status by UNESCO, affording them further protection.

The ascent of the mountain, particularly the western Naro Moru approach, can be attempted by anyone fit enough to jog a few kilometres. Although it is often the more adventurous tourist who climbs the mountain, provided the necessary precautions are taken, any healthy person can attempt the climb. The mountain's vegetation and geological features are so striking that any holiday in Kenya would be greatly impoverished by the omission of an ascent of Mount Kenya.

Mount Kenya's jagged peaks of Batian and Nelion (below) are whitened by a fresh dusting of snow. As the mountain is positioned astride the equator, early reports of snow by the German missionary Ludwig Krapf in 1849 were ridiculed by members of the learned circles in Europe, including David Livingstone. Krapf had to wait 34 years before his story was verified by the Scottish traveller, Joseph Thomson.

The heart of the mountain's spectacular upper Afro-alpine domain, with its prominent glacial features, is the volcanic plug that has been weathered by wind and ice to form the peaks of Batian and Nelion. The summit of Batian, at 5 199 metres, is 796 metres lower than that of Kilimanjaro. However, Batian still presents a challenge to most climbers. On most mornings, cloud obscures the high peaks and the mountain's jagged teeth only appear around midday. With the cloud lifted, the upper Teleki Valley is transformed into a scene of great beauty.

Altitude determines five distinct vegetation zones on the mountain. The extensive Afro-montane forest, covering the lower slopes, includes trees such as camphor, yellowwood and pencil-cedar. A zone of the impenetrable giant mountain bamboo replaces this forest, and above the bamboo the *Hagenia-Hypericum* forest occurs. As hagenia trees can better withstand cold and fire, they are able to outcompete other species and form almost pure stands above the bamboo. As the hagenia forest ends, a subalpine moorland of sedges and coarse tussock grasses begins. The tree heath, *Erica arborea*, is common at this altitude, as are helichrysums and gladioli. Above the moors, travellers enter the botanical marvel of the Afro-alpine zone. Situated on the equator, the length of day remains fairly constant throughout the year. As a result giganticism has occurred, and many species of alpine plants, such as lobelias and senecios, represented by herbs and forbs on other high mountains, often exceed 10 metres in height.

Although the harsh climatic conditions of the Afro-alpine region limit the number of plants to about 200 species, the remarkable adaptations displayed make this the most interesting of the mountain's plant zones. Lobelias and groundsels are the most conspicuous. The *Lobelia deckenii*, endemic to Mount Kenya, is recognized by its tall, erect flower that can attain a height of seven metres. *Lobelia telekii*, the 'ostrich plume plant', is an attractive, soft furry species that grows to four metres in height. The water-filled lobelia is a plant shaped like a rosette that grows close to the ground. At night when the water in the plant freezes, the ice prevents the cold from penetrating deeper and destroying the plant's central bud. Groundsels, closely related to grassland forbs, grow to astonishing heights. The candelabra-shaped tree groundsel grows to a height of over 10 metres and is the most conspicuous plant of the upper Afro-alpine reaches. The cabbage groundsel produces a cluster of yellow flowers only once in 20 years. Apart from these botanical oddities, the tree heath grows to the size of a small tree, as does a species of everlasting flower, *Helichrysum brownei*. Altogether, 13 plant species are unique to Mount Kenya. Mountain wildlife, too, varies with the altitude. The lower forests are home to elephant, buffalo, giant forest hog, bushpig, waterbuck, bushbuck, black-fronted duiker, leopard, Sykes' monkey and the black-and-white colobus monkey. Birdlife includes Hartlaub's Turaco, Jackson's Francolin, Bronze-naped Pigeon, Abyssinian Ground Thrush, Trumpeter Hornbill and many others. Once on the high moors, wildlife is less common. Animals that are permanently resident in this higher zone include smaller creatures such as shrews, hares, duiker, hyrax and klipspringer, as well as the magnificent stealthy leopard. These elusive predators have been sighted at altitudes as high as 4 600 metres on several occasions, and the carcass of an elephant was once found at the same altitude. At extreme altitude, only the groove-toothed rat – and humans temporarily – can survive in the harsh environment.

*T*o the west of the temperate central highlands, the land plunges steeply to the dry floor of the Great Rift Valley. A mere 25 kilometres separate the Aberdare heights from Lake Naivasha. But where the Cape chestnut and hagenia stood in misty glades, yellow-fever acacias add colour to the dry savanna. Rainfall here is much less, sometimes as little as a third of that measured on the Aberdares. Most people are more likely to see the Rift Valley for the first time along the road approaching the valley's edge, northwest of Nairobi. From the wooden platforms, located conveniently near the roadside curio stalls, the land below is a chequerboard of greens and browns. In the middle distance is Mount Longonot, a dormant volcano that surrounds an impressive crater. Nearby, Lake Naivasha is the closest body of water to Nairobi and a popular venue for weekend boating. The lake is rich in birdlife, yellow-fever trees crowd the shore, and the high walls of the Mau Escarpment and the imposing mass of Longonot add to its charm. Joy Adamson's house Elsamere, on the southern shore, is now run as a conservation centre. Teas and lunches are served on the lawns set under giant yellow-fever trees, and a troop of black-and-white colobus monkeys is normally present. These monkeys are spectacular to watch, as they leap from tree to tree with great agility. At the nearby Sulmac estate, about 4 000 people are employed in producing cut flowers. Once cut, the flowers are airfreighted to markets in Europe on the same day. On the southern shore of Lake Naivasha, the now-subdued Djinn Palace overlooking the lake was once the infamous haunt of settlers of *White Mischief* notoriety.

The flower of the lobelia (above) can grow to seven metres in height. On high mountains in other parts of the world, this genus is represented by small herbs and forbs. However, on the equator, hours of sunlight remaining fairly constant throughout the year engender strange and gigantic plants.

The Djinn Palace (below) on the southern shores of Lake Naivasha was once the retreat of the notoriously self-indulgent 'Happy Valley' white settlers. Today, the lake is known for its sizable flower farms, Africa's first geothermal power station, and Joy Adamson's former home, Elsamere, now run as a conservation centre.

Two of the five lakes in Kenya's central Rift Valley are protected: Nakuru and Bogoria. Lake Nakuru National Park covers 188 square kilometres and was the first park in Africa established to protect birdlife. Lesser Flamingos colour the bays a deep pink. The flamingos do not nest on the lake, but raise their young at Lake Natron, 200 kilometres to the south in Tanzania. Greater Flamingos are also present. The introduction of a species of tilapia fish in 1960 to control mosquitoes has attracted large numbers of pelicans, cormorants and other waterbirds. The lake and adjacent escarpment and acacia woodland have been enclosed by an electric fence erected to protect some 35 black rhino, and several white rhino donated by South Africa. Leopards are frequently seen, and other animals include Rothschild's giraffe – translocated from western Kenya – Grant's or plains zebra, waterbuck, reedbuck, eland, buffalo, lion and hippo. Visitors can stay at Lake Nakuru Lodge or Lion Hill Lodge, or at several picturesque campsites. Situated 60 kilometres to the north of Lake Nakuru, Lake Bogoria is the most dramatic of the central Rift Valley lakes. The wall of the Great Rift Valley rises a spectacular 630 metres above the flamingo-flecked waters, and hot springs erupt on its western shore. A 107-square-kilometre national reserve protects the lake and surrounding dry bush. A variety of wildlife including Grant's zebra, gazelle, and impala can be seen, and the reserve is the best site in Kenya for observing the greater kudu.

*I*n southern Kenya, to the east of the Rift Valley on the dry plains of Maasailand and close to the Tanzanian border, another awe-inspiring scene awaits the visitor. From Nairobi the tarred surface of either the A104 or A109 crosses the Athi and Kapiti plains, still grazed by large herds of Grant's zebra, kongoni and gazelle, and heads south towards Tanzania, or east towards Mombasa. Either route can be followed. The southern A104 leads past the Maasai district council capital at Kajiado. Much of the surrounding Maasailand consists of semi-arid grassland with scattered acacia trees. Home to some 300 000 Maasai and, in good years, about two million cattle, the 40 000 square kilometres of Maasailand is the last retreat for a tribe that was once the dominant power in East Africa.

The Maasai are thought to have migrated southwards from the Nile Valley in Sudan about 500 years ago. In the 1890s the rinderpest epidemic killed the cattle, and smallpox killed the people. The Maasai were later displaced from the Laikipia district by the colonial government and given the land in southern Kenya in perpetuity. Tall and slender, dressed in red and carrying little more than their long spears, Maasai herders are most often found in the company of their cherished cattle. Maasai society is founded on cattle ownership, and their language includes dozens of names for variations in cattle coloration or patterns. Since the first Europeans encountered the Maasai, accounts of the young warriors or *moran* spearing lions have elevated the Maasai's reputation to an almost mythical level, one that has been sustained by their habit of drinking milk mixed with cattle blood. The *eunoto* ceremony, during which a new set of *moran* graduates to become junior elders, and a new group of young men takes their place, has helped to enhance this reputation. The Maasai have, however, always respected wildlife. Apart from lion, speared by the *moran* as a test of manhood, they hunted buffalo and eland only during times of drought. It is no coincidence then that two of Kenya's principal wildlife reserves – Masai Mara National Reserve and Amboseli National Reserve – are situated on Maasailand.

The Maasai live in an *enkang*, or 'settlement', consisting of several low mud-and-dung-covered dwellings surrounded by a protective fence of thorn branches inside which the cattle are kept at night. Although the Maasai are still strict pastoralists, in some regions they now lease land to wheat farmers. Most Maasai are resistant to change and strongly protective of their culture, but some, such as Kenyan vice president George Saitoti, have entered the business or political arena.

At Kajiado the road crosses the railway that descends steeply westwards to the sunbaked depression containing the soda wasteland of Lake Magadi. Each year some 240 000 tons of soda ash, used in glass manufacturing, are extracted from the desolate lake and exported. The supply of soda is continuously replenished by subterranean hot springs.

*A*fter journeying 87 kilometres south of Kajiado across the acacia savanna, the road turns left at the border town of Namanga and leads across the dusty plain to Amboseli National Reserve. In a region that receives an average rainfall of 400 millimetres per year, the name Amboseli, a corruption of the Maasai word *empusel*, or 'salty dust', seems most appropriate. If the air is clear, Kilimanjaro's Uhuru peak rises magnificently into the sky. Even if the day is cloudy, the pastel-shaded slopes of the dormant volcano, punctuated in parts by cones produced by small lava vents, overshadow the thorny scrub of the plain.

Lake Nakuru (above), the first national park established in Africa for the conservation of birds, can support up to 1.5 million Lesser Flamingos. The flamingos feed on the blue-green *Spirulina* algae that thrive in the lake's alkaline water. Strangely, the flamingos do not breed at Lake Nakuru but raise their chicks at Lake Natron, 200 kilometres to the south. Besides its teeming birdlife, Lake Nakuru is an important sanctuary for rare animals such as Rothschild's giraffe, and both black and white rhino.

Kenya has 44 land-based national parks and national reserves, and an additional nine marine reserves. The parks of the Maasailand savanna – Amboseli, Nairobi and Masai Mara – each receive over 120 000 visitors a year. Located 220 kilometres south of Nairobi, Amboseli is the most accessible of Kenya's major reserves. The high concentration of tourists on the park's modest 392 square kilometres of fragile savanna is problematic. Consequently, the Kenya Wildlife Service has been forced to close off certain areas in order to limit the damage caused to the lake bed's fine soils by tourist vehicles.

Despite the aridity, however, springs originating on Mount Kilimanjaro's higher slopes reappear in the ancient lake bed to form lush swamps that attract an assortment of wild animals. Due to the beautiful setting, several of Hollywood's African yarns have been filmed on location at Amboseli. The cabins at Ol Tukai, now rented out by the Kajiado district council, were built as part of the set for the 1948 movie *The Snows of Kilimanjaro*. Nearby, Kilimanjaro Safari Lodge and Amboseli Lodge provide more upmarket accommodation. Amboseli Serena Lodge is located a few kilometres further south at the edge of the Enkongo Narok swamp.

In the 1970s it appeared as if the very geographical components that produced such splendour also contained the ingredients of its downfall – Amboseli became the scene of conflict between the people and the wildlife of the area. In 1948, a 3 260-square-kilometre triangle along the Tanzanian border was set aside as the Amboseli National Reserve. The boundary was arbitrarily drawn, not with a view to enclosing a viable ecosystem, but simply to place the Amboseli basin roughly in the centre of the reserve. The resident Maasai and their herds of livestock were allowed to remain. Maasai cattle depended on natural sources of water, and when waterholes dried up in times of drought, thousands would perish. However, the colonial authorities drilled boreholes and introduced vaccines to combat cattle diseases, and the number of cattle increased rapidly throughout Maasailand. Consequently, during the dry season, as many as 2 000 Maasai herders and 26 000 head of livestock made use of the central basin. It was not unusual for cattle herds to comprise 75 per cent of the biomass, while at the same time 75 per cent of the Kajiado district council's income came from visiting tourists.

The resident Maasai argued that they received no direct benefit from the income generated by tourism, as all the money was paid to the Kajiado council. To demonstrate their dissatisfaction with this arrangement, herders began spearing black rhino and elephant in protest. Poachers also played a role, and black rhino decreased from about 150 in 1950 to 30 in 1973, and 8 in 1977. The unique strain of long-horned black rhino, for which Amboseli was especially famous, was eliminated. The number of elephant decreased from 602 in 1973 to 478 in 1978. In an attempt to find a solution, David Western (now head of the Kenya Wildlife Service) began an investigation into the complexities of Amboseli in 1967. He found that during the wet season the wildlife of the Amboseli National Reserve became dispersed over an area of 5 000 square kilometres shared by 6 000 Maasai, 48 000 cattle, and 18 000 goats and sheep. During the Kenyan dry season, 80 per cent of wildlife concentrated in the 600 square kilometres of the central basin.

In response to the ongoing clash of interests and widespread deterioration of the habitat, the Kenyan government decided to act. By a presidential decree, 488 square kilometres of the central basin was proclaimed a national park, but it was accepted that the Maasai would not be displaced without adequate compensatory water and grazing. The Kajiado council retained control over 160 hectares at Ol Tukai, and the Maasai were granted title to grazing lands surrounding the park. Ownership of the grazing lands was achieved by dividing the land into group ranches organized along clan lines. The Maasai would withdraw from the park by 1977, and after withdrawing would receive a guarantee of adequate water supplies outside the park's boundaries, and annual compensation for losses sustained in accommodating wildlife.

A portion of swamp was later excised to give the Maasai additional dry-season pasture, and the final boundary enclosed 392 square kilometres of the central basin. Financed by the World Bank, Kenyan government and New York Zoological Society, a water pipeline was completed in 1977, directing water from a spring in the centre of the park to a series of water tanks north of the park. Wildlife herds benefited from the changes and a considerable increase in the population of Grant's zebra, wildebeest and buffalo was noted. During previous droughts, many young elephant had died as they had to compete for grazing with the herds of cattle. After the removal of cattle, the number of elephant increased by 30 per cent over five years. The number of black rhino also increased and group ranch elders helped the park authorities to identify poachers. The removal of Maasai settlements from the park also meant that a greater area of the park could now be used for grazing. The scheme worked well for a few years, but payments to the Maasai were often erratic. During the dry years, the water pipeline was unable to deliver sufficient water and the Maasai once again drove 10 000 cattle into the park.

A Maasai woman in southern Kenya (above). The Maasai drive large herds of cattle across the semi-arid savannas. Before the formation of nation states in Africa, the Maasai were nomadic pastoralists but an expanding population and pressures on land have forced many Maasai to become sedentary.

Mount Kilimanjaro (below), Africa's highest peak, is to the metre exactly two-thirds the height of Everest. Its snow-crowned summit towers above the arid plains of Amboseli, creating the archetypal safari portrait. Amboseli receives a low average rainfall – about 400 millimetres of rain per year.

Cheetah (above) are fairly easy to spot in the open grassland savannas of the Masai Mara. Over much of Africa, human population pressures and overhunting have reduced cheetah numbers. Cheetah are timid animals and limit competition with other predators such as lion and leopard by hunting during the heat of the day. Cheetah lack the powerful jaws of other predators and kill prey by strangulation.

In recent years the bureaucracy that existed in the government's Ministry of Tourism and Wildlife has been replaced by the restructured Kenya Wildlife Service. The service has shown itself to be a far more flexible and responsive organization, and under a revenue-sharing scheme, 25 per cent of gate receipts are now paid to the surrounding community. Schools, cattle bomas and dips have been built on nearby ranches. In poorly developed districts, such as those surrounding Amboseli, these contributions represent significant improvements for the community.

Cynthia Moss, a widely respected authority on elephants, has been gathering a wealth of information on elephant behaviour since 1972, and can recognize each of Amboseli's 790 elephants. Some researchers would argue that a population of 790 elephants is too large for Amboseli's fragile habitat. Large tracts of damaged or dead yellow-fever trees are evident along the swamp margins. However, David Western concluded that many of the trees had been killed by fluctuations in water-table levels that brought salts to the surface. Whatever the verdict might be, Cynthia Moss remains a fierce opponent of any cropping proposal, and the Amboseli elephants are among the best protected in Kenya.

Apart from the damage caused by elephant, an increase in tourist traffic could mar the very features that entice visitors to Amboseli. The lake bed's fine soils are easily eroded by continuous traffic and vehicles have had to be restricted to the roads. Excessive vehicle activity has had a marked impact on cheetah hunting behaviour, and evidence suggests that they now hunt during the daylight hours when visitors are lunching beside the lodge pool. The concentration of three lodges at Ol Tukai has also resulted in unsightly development, but the Kenya Wildlife Service cannot act as the land is controlled by the Kajiado council. However, despite Amboseli's problems past and present, the green haven of Ol Okenya swamp, its elephant herds feeding knee-high in the lush vegetation set before the wall of distant Kilimanjaro, will continue to remain a memorable highlight of any safari to Kenya.

West across the Great Rift Valley, 250 kilometres by small plane from Ol Tukai, there is a grassy plain wedged between the forested Loita Hills to the east and the 400-metre-high Soit Oloololo Escarpment to the west. The 1 500-square-kilometre Masai Mara National Reserve occupies less than four per cent of all Kenya's parks, and a mere seven per cent of the greater Serengeti-Mara ecosystem that falls mainly within neighbouring Tanzania. The Serengeti-Mara ecosystem is extremely productive. From a combination of factors the system is able to support an annual average of 100 wild animals per square kilometre. In most parts of Africa, grassland is associated with low rainfall or high altitude. The carrying capacity of the system and its ability to support grazers remains low, but in the Serengeti-Mara rainfall is high. In the Mara, rainfall can exceed 1 200 millimetres a year and falls during two rainy seasons: from November to January and March to May. With such high rainfall, the region should be covered by dense woodland, but chemical reactions in the soils underlying the grassland create an impenetrable hardpan that prevents deep-rooted trees from establishing themselves, while on the tall grassland, fires are able to limit the spread of woodland. The recent movement of elephant into the Serengeti-Mara ecosystem – approximately 1 300 occur in the Mara alone – also helps maintain grassland, and in many woodland areas, is converting the vegetation cover into grassland.

The annual wildebeest migration begins in the driest part of the ecosystem, on the short-grass plains near the Ngorongoro Crater in Tanzania. The wildebeest calve in January or February, and at the end of the rains in May, the herds leave these plains and migrate north into the tall-grass plains. The herds trek through the northern woodland of the Serengeti and arrive in the Mara from July onwards. Once the rains begin in the north in November, and the thunderstorm fronts begin to move south at a rate of 20 kilometres a day, the wildebeest complete the cycle and return to the short-grass plains. Each year 1.4 million wildebeest, 200 000 Grant's zebra, and 18 000 eland take part in this circular 500-kilometre journey. An estimated 500 000 Thomson's gazelle and 50 000 Grant's gazelle also migrate, but not to the same extent as the other species. The wildebeest migration into the Mara is a relatively recent occurrence. In the 1880s rinderpest was introduced to East Africa by livestock brought from Europe. Wildebeest, buffalo and cattle were virtually eliminated in many regions. In 1958 zoologists Bernhard and Michael Grzimek counted 99 000 wildebeest on the Serengeti. Between 1961 and 1963 the population rose by 40 per cent, and by 1977 was estimated at 1.4 million, a sixfold increase since 1962. After the Maasai cattle were inoculated against rinderpest, the disease disappeared from the system and the wildebeest population increased rapidly as a result. Prior to 1969, the migration did not extend as far north as the Mara. Now, over 700 000 wildebeest flood into the reserve, creating an annual phenomenon that has become Kenya's foremost wildlife spectacle.

An interesting consequence of the concentration of game in the Mara is that dry-season fires are now rare. In the Maasai language, *mara* means 'spotted', a reference to the acacia-dotted grassland. After the rinderpest epidemic, thickets and woodland encroached on the grassland and the Maasai referred to the Mara as *osere*, meaning 'thick bush'. Researchers have found that the migratory herds benefit from the grassland and the trampling caused by several million hooves for three months of the year actually discourages the growth of tree seedlings. A mutually beneficial relationship therefore exists between the grazers and the grassland. Apart from migratory animals, the reserve also provides dry-season grazing for about 100 000 wildebeest from the Loita population. Animals that occur through-

out the year on the plains include buffalo, topi, kongoni, gazelle, eland and giraffe. The Mara's greatest drawcard is the concentration of predators on the open plains. Visitors to the Masai Mara are bound to come across the big cats – there are approximately 3 000 lion and 1 000 cheetah in the entire ecosystem. It is more difficult to find a leopard, but other predators that can be seen in the Mara include spotted hyena, striped hyena, wild dog, black-backed jackal, golden jackal, bat-eared fox, serval, caracal, civet and honey badger. Although the population of black rhino has been greatly reduced throughout Africa, the Mara can still claim to be 'big five' country. Between 30 to 40 black rhinos inhabit the area, and 10 white rhinos were imported from South Africa in September 1994.

In 1977, political tensions between Kenya and Tanzania resulted in the border post in the southern Mara being closed. With this closure, more tourists came to the Masai Mara. The three existing lodges and camps – Keekorok, Mara Serena and Governors' – no longer provided sufficient accommodation. Today there are seven lodges and 12 tented camps in the Mara region, eight of which are located within the boundaries of the reserve. The Mara has developed into one of the most renowned wildlife destinations in Africa and each year attracts about 154 000 visitors.

*T*o the east of Amboseli, on either side of the main Nairobi to Mombasa road and railway, the Tsavo National Park covers 21 283 square kilometres of arid savanna – an area larger than Wales or Massachusetts. Tsavo is Kenya's largest national park and the fifth largest in Africa. Divided for administrative purposes into Tsavo West and Tsavo East, and the adjacent Chyulu Hills, Tsavo's boundary embraces 83 per cent of all national park land in Kenya. Each year, 240 000 visitors are lured to Tsavo for its diverse wildlife, vast wilderness, rugged scenery, and the comfort offered by the park's eight game lodges and tented camps. Much of Tsavo's appeal lies in the juxtaposition of sharp contrasts: broad plains yield to volcanic hills or lava flows; parched hills surround the crystal-clear waters of Mzima Springs; the Tsavo and Athi rivers cut verdant ribbons across arid plains; and reed-fringed Lake Jipe is dwarfed by the white summit of Kilimanjaro.

While only the southern third of Tsavo East National Park (south of the Galana River) is open to the public, Tsavo West National Park is crisscrossed by dozens of tracks, each one of which is conveniently marked by a numbered cairn. Within easy reach of Kitani Safari Camp and Kilanguni Lodge, Mzima Springs is perhaps the park's chief attraction. A genuine oasis, Mzima Springs' pools of clear water originate in the volcanic Chyulu Hills, 25 kilometres to the north, where rain soaking into the porous lava re-emerges at the springs. The filtered water has created a palm- and fever-tree-fringed oasis inhabited by hippo, crocodile, waterbirds and fish. An underwater hide situated at the springs provides visitors with rare glimpses of the submarine habitats. Nearby, an unobtrusive 200-kilometre pipeline taps water from the springs, providing Mombasa with most of its water requirements.

During the annual migration (above) across the Serengeti Plain in Tanzania, over 800 000 wildebeest and 40 000 plains zebra spill over into the Masai Mara National Reserve in Kenya where they are forced to cross the Mara River. Although zebra usually cross the river without incident, the wildebeest do not fare as well and in some years many drown during the crossing.

A **monument** (above) at the site within Nairobi National Park where a 12-ton pile of ivory was torched (below) by President Moi in July 1989, after rampant poaching in the 1980s threatened the survival of Kenya's elephants. At a meeting of CITES members in Switzerland in October 1989, the worldwide trade in elephant products was banned.

Thirteen kilometres north, the inhospitable wasteland of the Shetani lava flow ('Shetani' means 'devil' in Kiswahili) is a marked contrast to the cool tranquillity of Mzima. Thought to have erupted only 200 years ago, the Shetani lava field is further evidence of recent volcanic activity in this corner of Kenya. Besides Tsavo's volcanic hills and broad savannas, its herds of game, and some 400 species of birds, the park is in many ways a microcosm of the complex issues facing conservationists in Africa. In the early 1970s Tsavo could boast the third largest protected elephant population in Africa. The rise and fall of Tsavo's elephant, and the transformation of the impenetrable *nyika* thickets of commiphora and acacia into open savanna, has been well documented. In several southern African countries elephant are cropped once they exceed a predetermined carrying capacity, but in Tsavo National Park the wardens adhered to a strict noninterference policy. The elephant population was allowed to increase entirely unchecked and the profound changes in vegetation that followed were regarded as being part of the natural cycle.

Archaeological findings suggest that since the sixteenth century Maasai and Orma pastoralists, Kamba hunters and pastoralists, Taita hunters, and Watta nomadic elephant hunters all made use of Tsavo. By the 1890s, however, a rinderpest epidemic critically reduced both the number and the range of these societies. By 1930 the tribes had recovered and conflicting land claims began to emerge. The Kenya Land Commission of 1933 divided land into 'native reserve' and 'crown land'. The former classification applied where long-standing tribal claims existed, the latter where land was lightly settled or seemingly devoid of any firm claim. Besides the land allocated to the Maasai by treaty, the commission did not accommodate nomadic pastoralists, although grazing rights were granted in some instances.

In April 1948 the Tsavo National Park was established. The earlier grazing rights awarded by the land commission to pastoralists were ignored. David Sheldrick and Bill Woodley were appointed to manage the 11 747-square-kilometre parched expanse of Tsavo East. In the park's early years, as recorded by Daphne Sheldrick, browsers such as lesser kudu, dik-dik and gerenuk were the most common animals. Buffalo, eland and Grant's zebra were only occasionally glimpsed in small scattered groups, and waterbuck and impala were restricted to the rivers. The rather haggard Tsavo lions were found singly or in pairs. Predictably, elephant outnumbered all other species in terms of biomass. In 1957, David Sheldrick's first aerial census of Tsavo East counted between 2 000 and 4 000 elephant. In 1962 the count for the whole region totalled 16 000, but by 1969 the population exceeded 40 000.

In 1970 to 1971 Tsavo suffered under a severe drought. At least 9 000 elephant and 600 black rhino perished. Not only did the surrounding people benefit from an abundance of easily harvested ivory but with much of the bush now cleared by elephant, poaching became a serious problem. Somali poachers, armed with automatic weapons, slaughtered on average three elephants a day. By 1988 Tsavo's elephant population had collapsed to 6 000; the national total had decreased from 167 000 in 1973 to 20 000 in 1989. An even worse fate awaited the black rhino. In 1969 Tsavo contained between 6 000 and 9 000 black rhino, the largest population in Africa, while the estimate for Kenya was 20 000. Once the thickets had been destroyed, it was a simple task for poachers to track down the rhino. A 1977 census revealed that there were only 1 500 animals left, and by 1989 only a small remnant remained.

Richard Leakey publicly accused the Ministry of Tourism and Wildlife of mismanagement and corruption – elephant in Tsavo were frequently poached near the ranger posts, by the very rangers employed to protect them, and ivory dealers in Hong Kong were known to deposit funds into a New York account registered in the name of the ministry. President Moi responded by appointing Leakey to head the restructured Kenya Wildlife Service. Leakey succeeded in securing US$140 million in grants from overseas donors. The rangers' antiquated .303 rifles were replaced with automatic weapons, Land-Rovers and airplanes were donated, and even military helicopters were loaned by the British army. In July 1989, President Daniel arap Moi symbolically set fire to an enormous 12-ton pile of ivory that was valued at US$3 million near the entrance to Nairobi National Park. In October 1989, the African elephant was transferred from Appendix II to Appendix I, a reclassification by CITES that banned the worldwide import or export of elephant products. Several southern African countries applied for exemption from the ivory ban, but by the next CITES meeting in 1992, there was widespread acceptance of the vital need to continue the ban on ivory trade in Kenya as well as in other African countries.

Within two years the ivory ban succeeded in reducing the price a poacher received for raw ivory from US$50 per kilogram to US$3 per kilogram. Elephants in Tsavo have increased to 7 500, and the Kenyan total now stands at around 25 000. Prior to 1989 poachers were killing 1 000 elephants per year in Tsavo; in 1990 and 1991 no deaths were reported; in 1992, six elephants were poached, 14 in 1993. In the first seven months of 1994, no losses were reported. The black rhino population, although still dangerously low, has also been stabilized. Rhinos are now protected inside electrified sanctuaries, such as at Ngulia in Tsavo West. In 1994, 421 black rhino were to be found in Kenya, 44 of them in Tsavo.

It has been argued that Tsavo's irregular boundaries never enclosed an ecological unit, only a political one. When the park was proclaimed, the Watta (the nomadic elephant hunters of Tsavo) were excluded from the park's management plan. Not only was their ecological role misunderstood but the expulsion of people from land they had utilized for generations before it was earmarked for conservation is an example of the kind of blunder committed by many a colonial government in Africa. The challenge that faces conservation in Kenya is to ensure that the parks benefit the surrounding population. Kenya now sustains 13 million cattle, eight million goats, 6.5 million sheep, and about 1.5 million head of game. A quarter of gate revenues from parks such as Tsavo is paid to adjacent communities. An increase in tourist receipts, therefore, directly benefits the people who have to bear the greatest cost – the Maasai herders whose goats are killed by predators, and the smallholders whose crops are destroyed by elephant.

*T*here are many Arcadian tropical islands and uncrowded, palm-lined beaches in the world. Kenya's coast, protected by coral reefs for almost its entire length, is not uncharacteristic of Indian Ocean coastlines. Nevertheless, since the mid-1970s the coastal strip has become Kenya's prime tourist destination. Apart from a choice of about 50 hotels, the Kenyan coast boasts a magnificent coral reef, ancient ruins, remote islands, uncharted mangrove swamps, and a blend of Arab, African, Asian and European cultures that dates back to the Middle Ages.

The Kenyan coast stretches for about 700 kilometres from Wasini Island, near the Tanzanian border, to Kiunga, alongside Somalia. The most popular beaches can be found along the 90-kilometre road south of Mombasa to Shimoni, or north along the 120-kilometre route to the ancient town of Malindi. Much of the Kenyan coast's attraction is due to the coral reefs that stretch from north of Malindi southwards to Shimoni. Not only do the reefs safeguard the beaches from pounding waves and strong currents but they also prevent sharks from coming close to the shore.

Taking the overnight train from Nairobi is a popular way of travelling to Mombasa. The train journey ends at the station in the centre of Mombasa Island. The core of the city is the five-kilometre-long by four-kilometre-wide island bordered by the deep chan-

A pair of gigantic aluminium tusks (above) frames the entrance to the town of Mombasa. The adjacent sidewalk is densely packed with curio stalls, each one competing for the passing tourist trade. Central Mombasa occupies an island five kilometres long and four kilometres wide. As the island is surrounded by a large convoluted bay, it was the perfect site for a port city in ancient times as it offered both protection from hostile tribes from the interior, while allowing for trade with the Persian Gulf, India and China.

nel of Kilindini harbour to the south and Port Tudor to the north. Many of the rusty-roofed buildings on the island are over a hundred years old, those in the 'Old Town' sector even older. The heat and humidity, the maze of streets dividing ragged and unimaginative apartment blocks, sidewalks crammed with hawkers, and a generally squalid and unsavoury appearance, convey a slightly different impression from that presented in guidebooks. However, as the Swahili proverb *Nyumba mjema si mlango* says, 'a good house is not judged by its appearance', and this is very true of Mombasa – there is much in this city to interest the visitor.

Unlike the majority of large African cities that were established during the colonial period, settlement patterns on the Kenyan coast date back thousands of years. Initial links between the coastal settlements and the hinterland were hampered by the difficult terrain. The annual monsoon winds encouraged trade links with the Persian Gulf, Arabia, India and even China. From November to March the northeast wind brought merchants from Asia in search of ivory, rhino horn, coconut oil and spices. In exchange, they traded ceramics, glass, metal objects and wheat. When the wind changed direction from April to October, the merchants would sail their dhows back to the Persian Gulf.

By the eighth and ninth centuries Arabs had settled along the coast. The colonizers chose offshore islands, such as the northern islands of Lamu, Pate and Manda, as they offered security against possible attacks from the mainland tribes. By the twelfth century prosperous trading settlements had become established on the islands. The ruins of one of the oldest coastal settlements, Takwa, can still be seen on Manda Island. The town was a thriving community until it was mysteriously abandoned in the seventeenth century. Houses were built facing Mecca, the town had a mosque, and an inscription

A cross (above) of Lisbon limestone was erected in Malindi in January 1499 by the Portuguese mariner Vasco da Gama, after he was warmly welcomed by the sultan of Malindi. It is situated on a peninsula overlooking the broad curve of Malindi's bay. The Portuguese maintained a presence on the coast for much of the seventeenth century, but little trace of this period of occupation remains today.

Dhows lie anchored (above) along the seawall of ancient Lamu's waterfront. Lamu's busy centre of activity is its waterfront and adjoining town centre, which can be explored along a maze of narrow streets. The remote north coast island is a popular retreat for visitors seeking seclusion and an experience out of the ordinary.

on one of the strange pillar tombs found only along the coast dates to about 1680. The inhabitants lived in large houses built from coral, and traded commodities such as ivory, tortoiseshell, leopard skins and gold. Surrounded by a wall, and with a mangrove swamp on one side and the sea on the other, the town would have been easy to defend. To date no clue revealing the cause of the evacuation has been found.

The Shirazi Arabs from the Persian Gulf began to settle on the coast from about the twelfth century. They intermarried with the local Africans and within a few generations formed a new group, the Swahili people. Although never numerous, they soon became the ruling class along the coast. Many of their ancient coastal settlements now lie abandoned, ruined by the passage of time and the encroachment of the jungle while the language that arose has endured. The word 'Swahili' is derived from the Arabic *sahel*, meaning 'coast'. The Arab influence on Swahili culture is apparent in its architecture, pottery and Islamic religion, the African in the Kiswahili language. Essentially an African language that borrowed heavily from Arabic, Portuguese, Indian languages and even English, Kiswahili was later carried into the interior by the trade caravans and slave traders. Today it is the lingua franca over much of East Africa, and even as far afield as eastern Zaïre.

In 1498 the Portuguese explorer Vasco da Gama sailed into Mombasa during a voyage in search of a sea route to India. Portugal was anxious to find a trade route that would avoid the obstacle, raised by the Ottoman Turks, to trade with the Far East. The Portuguese received an unfriendly reception from the people of Mombasa. They sailed on to Malindi where they received a warmer welcome from the sultan, a bitter enemy of Mombasa.

Four years later Da Gama returned briefly, but in 1505 Francisco d'Almeida arrived with a large fleet of ships and 1 500 men. Although the king of Mombasa had recruited 1 500 archers to ward off the expected attack, they could not compete against Portuguese firearms. Casualties at the end of the battle totalled five Portuguese and 1 513 citizens of Mombasa. The Portugeuse then plundered the town, and set sail. Mombasa was again attacked by the Portuguese on three occasions between 1528 and 1589. Despite all the years of turmoil, Mombasa was able to assemble a force and set off to attack Malindi in 1591. They were defeated and Mombasa was placed under the sovereignty of Sheik Ahmad of Malindi. The Portuguese returned and began building Fort Jesus in a strategic position overlooking the harbour. Most of the coastal cities fell under Portuguese jurisdiction, and for much of the seventeenth century they controlled the coast. But Portugal's power was diminishing, and the country had already become a vassal of Spain. In 1631 the people of Mombasa rebelled and captured Fort Jesus. Later, in 1696, Omani Arabs besieged the fort for nearly three years during which time all 1 500 defenders perished. Dissatisfied with their new Omani rulers, the locals rebelled in 1728 and the Portuguese returned. A year later the fort was again besieged. The Portuguese soon surrendered and set sail for the last time. Although the coastal settlements resisted Omani advances, the Sultan of Oman, Sayyid Said, with the necessary assistance of second-hand naval ships that were acquired from Britain, succeeded in capturing Mombasa in 1837. The coastal strip remained under Omani control until it was declared a British protectorate in 1895.

Despite their long association with the coast, little sign remains today of Portuguese occupation. Apart from crops such as corn, tomatoes, tobacco, cassava and cashews introduced from the Americas, and contributions to the Kiswahili vocabulary, tangible reminders of 230 years of Portuguese influence are limited to Vasco da Gama's *padrão* or cross, erected in 1499 at Malindi, and Fort Jesus. The imposing fort, its walls stained and worn by years of heat and rain, has outlived all its conquerors. A labyrinth of narrow streets and alleys crosses the adjacent Old Town. Shops around every corner sell carpets, brass, fabrics and spices from the Persian Gulf. Fishermen sell fish at the market in the square near the old harbour. Many of the surrounding buildings date back to nineteenth-century Zanzibari influence, but the ornate carved doors, fretwork balconies, protruding upper floors, and rusty iron roofs that mingle with the aroma of spices and the haunting sound of the muezzins' call to prayer are evocative of the town's Arab past.

On the south side of Mombasa Island, the twin Likoni ferries take four minutes to transport cargoes of cars, buses and pedestrians across the deep waters of Kilindini harbour. Once the mainland is reached, the smooth, palm-lined road runs down the south coast to Lungalunga on the Tanzanian border, passing the famous beaches of Tiwi, Diani and Shimoni. Fifteen kilometres inland at Kwale, the Shimba Hills National Reserve contains Kenya's only coastal game lodge; the wooden, five-storey Shimba Lodge faces a waterhole surrounded by coastal jungle. The 192 square kilometres of rolling grassy hills and forest provide panoramic views over the Indian Ocean and nearby Diani Beach. The reserve contains Kenya's only herds of sable antelope, an estimated 600 elephant, and waterbuck, bushbuck, Grant's zebra, monkeys and leopards.

Nearby, the 10-kilometre stretch of Diani Beach is acclaimed as East Africa's most popular coastal resort. At the northern end of the beach, the fifteenth-century Kongo Mosque, set in a grove of baobabs at the mouth of the Tiwi River, is all that remains of an earlier settlement. However, it is the palm-fringed beach protected by an offshore reef that attracts the most attention. Even at low tide, the water within the sanctuary formed by the reef is deep enough for swimming and snorkelling among the shoals of colourful tropical fish. The appeal of Diani's pure white sands and turquoise sea has encouraged developers, and visitors can choose from dozens of hotels and lodges.

Thirty kilometres south of Diani, just after the sugar cane fields of Ramisi, a sandy track leads directly to Shimoni Beach. A remote and rugged coastline, Shimoni is named after a fascinating cave (*shimo* in Kiswahili) that extends inland for 20 kilometres. Shimoni is Kenya's prime game-fishing venue, and the Pemba Channel Fishing Club and Shimoni Reef Fishing Lodge cater for serious anglers. Its major attraction, however, is a stretch of coastline that has been little affected by progress. Offshore, on the unspoilt five-square-kilometre Wasini Island, visitors can explore an ancient village, or enjoy superb seafood and Swahili cuisine, or simply relax and enjoy the sunshine on the beautiful beach. Just south of the island, a 39-square-kilometre rectangle of reef and ocean is protected within the Kisite Marine National Park and Mpunguti Marine National Reserve. The parks extend over coral reefs offering the best snorkelling in Kenya. Visitors can explore the parks from a dhow that sails from Wasini Island.

The northern B8 from Mombasa to Malindi is linked to the mainland by the Nyali bridge. At the Mtwapa and Kilifi creeks, drowned river valleys push the sea far inland, and in the past, the journey was prolonged by lengthy ferry crossings. Today, thanks to Japanese-built bridges, the north coast's beaches are within quick and easy reach. On the way to Mtwapa Creek, the idyllic Nyali, Bamburi and Shanzu beaches have the highest concentration of five-star hotels in Kenya. Offshore, the sea is protected within the 210-square-kilometre Mombasa Marine National Park and National Reserve, established in 1986. From Mtwapa Creek the road leads for 90 kilometres to Watamu. Near Watamu the road skirts the dense canopy of the 389-square-kilometre Arabuko-Sokoke forest, the largest surviving coastal forest in Kenya. The forest is home to a number of both fascinating and rare animals and birds, such as the Zanzibar duiker, golden-rumped elephant shrew, Clarke's Weaver, and the endemic Sokoke Scops Owl.

Along the road to Watamu, the ruins of the ancient town of Gedi are among the most mysterious of the coastal ruins, the town having been inexplicably abandoned in the sixteenth century. Located several kilometres from the sea, Gedi is characteristic of a medieval town in its layout. An inner and outer stone wall surrounded the central palace and six mosques, while an estimated 2 500 inhabitants lived beyond the walls.

Watamu is renowned for its scuba diving, snorkelling and deep-sea fishing. Watamu's main attraction is the adjacent marine reserve, the largest in Kenya. The reserve extends northwards to Malindi and seawards to the outer reef, conserving 261 square kilometres of the marine ecosystem, including the extensive Mida Creek lagoon. Within the Watamu Marine National Park that forms the core of the sanctuary, all sea life is strictly protected. The tar road ends at the ancient town of Malindi. The town is a curious mixture of narrow lanes, Swahili architecture and carved doors that merge with the white hotel façades and gift shops of a tourist resort. South of the town centre along the wide sands of Silversands Beach, resorts such as the Driftwood Club and Coconut Village attract many tourists of all nationalities, particularly Germans and Italians. Further south at Casuarina Point, glass-bottomed boats conduct regular excursions to explore the coral reefs of the six-square-kilometre Malindi Marine National Park. These trips are popular with the tourists. Surrounding the marine park, the national reserve extends five kilometres out to sea and 30 kilometres along the coast to Watamu.

North of Malindi, a decrease in rainfall and the delta of Kenya's largest river, the Tana, limits population density. Much of the surrounding vegetation is still intact and wild animals, including a few elephant, are still common. From Malindi, the dirt road leads to Mokowe on the mainland opposite the island of Lamu. Even if visitors arrive by plane, it is still necessary to cross by boat to Lamu. Located on the eastern side of the island, the port of Lamu has had trading links with the outside world since the ninth century. The oldest building, Pwani mosque, dates back to 1370. There is only one car on the island, and residents rely on donkeys and dhows for transport. The centre of attention is the town's waterfront adjoining the harbour. Decorated portals and balconies, carved wooden doors, and moulded plasterwork adjoin the sea wall. Lamu is crisscrossed by a maze of narrow streets that, from the air, makes the town look like a jigsaw puzzle. Peponi Hotel, on the southern side of the island at Shela, is a popular tourist venue.

A dhow enters Mombasa's old port (below), as they have done for many centuries. The first reference to the coastal ports dates back to Diogenes's account *The Periplus of the Erythraean Sea*, written in AD 110. Over the next 600 years, the Arabs settled along the coast. They established trading ports and rivalry between the towns was common. Intermarriage with coastal Africans resulted in the development of the Kiswahili language, which was later carried by trade caravans and slave traders into the interior. Today the language is still the lingua franca over much of East Africa.

At the Akamba woodcarving factory
in Mombasa (above), skilled carvers
practise a trade that was learned
during World War I from the Makonde
carvers of the coast of Tanzania.
Curios manufactured by the carvers
are displayed in roadside markets
throughout Kenya.

*I*nland from the coastal islands, the vast Northeastern Province stretches north along the border with Somalia. Although the province accounts for over one-fifth of Kenya's land area, the harsh desert accommodates about two per cent of the total population. Of Kenya's eight provinces, visitors are least likely to journey through this region. Kenya's only endemic antelope, Hunter's hartebeest, survives here in the dry bush of the Arawale National Reserve.

An estimated 72 per cent of Kenya receives an annual average rainfall of under 500 millimetres. The village of Wajir receives 232 millimetres. In the vicinity of Lake Turkana rainfall can be half this amount, while the annual evaporation often exceeds 2 600 millimetres. The vegetation of the Northeastern Province, and the regions of the eastern and Rift Valley provinces that extend into the arid north, consists primarily of scattered acacia and commiphora bushes. A scant covering of grass grows between the bushes, but during periods of prolonged drought grass may be absent for years. In the extreme north, near Ethiopia, the barren wasteland of the Chalbi Desert has partially resulted from the presence of an enclosed drainage basin. After meagre showers have fallen on higher ground, water flowing into the basin evaporates and brings salts to the surface, thereby preventing the growth of all but the most hardy of grasses. Isolated forests can also be found in the arid north. In a country of sudden contrasts, it is perhaps not too surprising to encounter forests on mountains such as Ndoto, the Matthews range and Marsabit, which in some places soar 1 800 metres above the surrounding desert. The most accessible of the desert forests can be found on Marsabit, 226 kilometres north of the frontier town of Archer's Post. An isolated mountain surrounded by parched desert, Marsabit, meaning 'place of cold', rises to a height of 1 722 metres above the Kaisut Desert. An extinct volcano, it has three fascinating craters that can be explored on the summit. The higher slopes of the mountain fall within the Marsabit National Park. The mountain's eastern slopes are dry and stark, but dense and verdant forest harbouring many forest animals and birds covers the western slopes of the mountain.

Strangely, precipitation on Marsabit originates from the bleak desert that encircles the mountain. Hot air rising from the surrounding desert condenses over the mountain, especially at night when temperatures fall. Rain and mist result and sustain the mountain's dense moss-festooned forest. Marsabit is famous for having been the home of the legendary elephant Ahmed, who, thanks to his enormous pair of tusks, was declared a national monument by President Kenyatta. Ahmed's skin was sent to a taxidermist and his preserved form now stands outside the National Museum in Nairobi. Other big tuskers still occur on the mountain, but apart from elephant, Marsabit harbours greater kudu, buffalo, monkeys, leopard, reticulated giraffe and Grevy's zebra. Birds of prey are represented by an impressive 52 species. From the 10-kilometre track that runs along the rim of the largest crater, Gof Bongole, the rare Bearded Vulture, or Lammergeier, can be spotted.

Across the wasteland that separates Marsabit from Lake Turkana to the west, the nomadic Rendille tribe, numbering about 20 000, follows a lifestyle that has been little influenced by the modern age. The Rendille are descendants of the earliest known migration of Cushitic-speaking people from the highlands of Ethiopia. They tended herds of goats, sheep and camels, and occupied those regions that were too arid for hunter-gatherer groups. They developed elaborate customs to manage such contentious issues as water rights, ownership and inheritance.

On the edge of Rendille territory, Lake Turkana is one of the most intriguing of Kenya's many natural wonders. The largest desert lake in the world, it measures 240 kilometres in length and occupies 6 400 square kilometres. Lying in the Rift Valley, the lake has no access to the sea, and yet the presence of the Nile perch indicates that a primeval link with the Nile has since been severed. The Omo River flows into the north of the lake from the Ethiopian highlands. Where the Omo enters the lake, a typical bird's-foot delta has been formed by silt-laden water flowing through a levee before depositing its load. There is geological evidence that the lake once extended 200 kilometres further south to Lake Baringo, which indicates a 150-metre drop in water level. As the system is closed, there is no outlet for the salts carried into the lake by rivers. As a result, the taste of the alkaline water is comparable to that of soda water. The dissolved salts colour the lake a marine green, and it has become known as the 'Jade Sea'.

Large numbers of waterbirds feed in the shallow waters adjoining the shoreline of Lake Turkana. The lake also harbours one of the largest surviving populations of Nile crocodile in Africa, estimated at over 10 000. Three national parks have been established on islands or along the northeastern shore. Some eight kilometres north of the village of Loiyangalani, a collection of huts covered with palm fronds situated on a particularly desolate plain of black gravel is the only indication that the visitor has reached the el-Molo tribe's sole village. The el-Molo have never been pastoralists, and depend entirely on fishing, occasionally hunting crocodile and hippo. Numbering only about 500 people, the el-Molo have been the subject of much curiosity in the past. It is thought that they migrated to the lake shore about 2 000 years ago. There has been speculation that the el-Molo descended from a Rendille group that was forced to fish after their livestock had perished. However, there is evidence to suggest that the el-Molo have always been fishermen.

On the western shore of the lake, the lithe, jet-black Turkana people inhabit the land rising to the escarpment adjoining the Ugandan border. The Turkana speak a language that is related to that of the Maasai and Samburu. Unlike many other pastoralist societies, the close proximity of Lake Turkana has led to their acceptance of fish as a source of protein. The Turkana maintain herds of sheep, goats, cattle and camels. Like the Rendille, the Turkana use camels as the desert equivalent of a milk cow, not as a means of transport. On the long road returning from Lake Turkana, the wooded slopes of the Nyiru Mountains provide a welcome relief from the harsh landscape of the barren desert. The Samburu village of South Horr, tucked in a narrow cleft between the mountains, has a splendid campsite dominated by gigantic acacia trees. The Samburu people are northern relatives of the Maasai people.

About 150 kilometres to the south, the Ewaso Nyiro River – Samburu for 'river of brown water' – carves a channel across the desert. The Ewaso Nyiro finally disappears in the Lorian Swamp, 300 kilometres short of the sea, its waters unable to sustain the journey across the scorched sands of the Sabena Desert. The river, lined by doum palms and riverine vegetation, meanders through a rugged landscape of hills and arid plains, and forms the boundary between three national reserves that have become well known in recent years through Joy Adamson's writings.

The 165-square-kilometre Samburu National Reserve and the 131-square-kilometre Buffalo Springs National Reserve are also known for their fascinating wildlife that includes oryx, gerenuk, dik-dik, reticulated giraffe and Grevy's zebra. The reserves are important ranges for the Grevy's zebra and contain about a quarter of the national total of 6 000. Elsewhere, only a few hundred survive in Ethiopia and this zebra has not been seen in Somalia since 1973. Other wild animals include approximately 200 elephant (often seen near the river), eland, gazelle, waterbuck, buffalo, cheetah and lion, which are frequently seen in Buffalo Springs. Leopard are common in the rocky terrain of Samburu and two riverside lodges, Samburu Lodge and Samburu Serena Lodge, place bait out every night to attract them. To the east, the 239-square-kilometre Shaba National Reserve was the site chosen by Joy Adamson for the release of the leopard, Penny. Shaba, or 'copper', is named after a copper-coloured sandstone mountain that overlooks the reserve The Ewaso Nyiro River cuts across the reserve, flowing through a series of gorges and rapids. In January 1980 Joy Adamson was murdered in Shaba. Her husband, George Adamson, continued his work with lions at Kora National Park, before he too was murdered by poachers in August 1989.

*I*n the heyday of colonial exploration, to find the source of the Nile, the world's longest river, became something of an obsession among explorers and academics alike. In 1768, a Scot named James Bruce set out from Egypt and after two years reached the source of the Blue Nile in Ethiopia. It was not until 1857 that a second serious attempt was made. In June 1857 Richard Burton and John Hanning Speke, along with 132 porters, left from Zanzibar. On 13 February 1858, with Speke partially blinded by disease and Burton suffering from malaria, the expedition reached Lake Tanganyika, which they believed to be the source of the Nile. But after they had explored the lake, they discovered that the Ruzizi River flowed into it from the north, and Tanganyika could therefore not be the source. However, Burton remained convinced that the Nile was fed by another outlet. Speke went on to explore Lake Nyanza, a lake that had been described by Arab slave traders and which Speke thought could, in fact, turn out to be what he was searching for – the source of the Nile. He reached the lake in August 1858 and named it after Queen Victoria. A sceptical Burton refused to accept Speke's claim, and the expedition returned to Zanzibar. A year later Speke undertook a second expedition, and explored a series of rapids on the lake's northern shore. Speke was convinced that he had found the Nile's source. Although Speke received a hero's welcome on his return to England, not everyone was convinced about his findings.

The brightly attired Samburu (above), closely related to the Maasai people, maintain a nomadic pastoralist existence on the arid lands that stretch north of the Ewaso Nyiro River towards Lake Turkana; their lifestyle has been little influenced by change. Visitors to game lodges in the Samburu National Reserve often have the opportunity of attending the Samburu's colourful dances.

A fish harvest (above) on Mfangano Island, Lake Victoria. Compared to many of the African Rift Valley lakes, Lake Victoria's waters are relatively shallow and yield large catches of tilapia and Nile perch.

A Pokot settlement (top) in the high Cheranganis, the forested highlands north of Eldoret that form the western edge of the Great Rift Valley.

The Royal Geographical Society was anxious to end the controversy, and commissioned David Livingstone to do so. After no word had been received from Livingstone for some time, the American journalist Henry Morton Stanley was sent after him. Stanley found Livingstone at Lake Tanganyika on 10 November 1871. Two years later David Livingstone died while searching for a southerly tributary of Lake Tanganyika. After Livingstone's death, Stanley was commissioned by the *New York Herald* and *London Daily Telegraph* to settle the dispute. He sailed around the shores of the lake, confirming that only one river flowed out of it. Stanley then took his party to unravel the mysteries of the Congo River. In a single expedition he succeeded in solving all the remaining riddles of Africa's waterways.

Scarcely a century later, ferries now carry passengers and cargo across Lake Victoria to nearby islands, and further afield to ports in Uganda and Tanzania. The lake is no longer a source of intrigue, and its islands and shoreline are now home to millions of people. Kisumu, at the head of Winam Gulf, is Kenya's third largest town and a major lake port. The region has changed much since 1902 when, after six years of construction, the 'Lunatic Line' finally reached the lake. Fishermen now fly in for a morning's fishing at Mfangano Island from camps in the Masai Mara. The largest freshwater fish in the world, the Nile perch (weighing up to 80 kilograms), and Nile tilapia are the chief enticements. Despite the change, Luo fishermen still sail their painted sailing dhows that have remained similar in design since the days of the Arab slave traders.

Apart from the lake, which lies at an altitude of 1 162 metres above sea level, and its surrounding drainage basin, much of the land in western Kenya lies above 1 500 metres. On the fertile highlands where rain can fall throughout the year, coffee, tea, wheat, timber, sugar and dairy products are significant contributors to the Kenyan economy. Fifty kilometres east of the lake, the town of Kericho is the centre of Kenya's tea industry. Kericho is ideally suited for tea production. Tea was first grown in the district in the 1920s from plants brought from India and Ceylon. Kenya is now the fourth largest producer of tea in the world, and Kenyan tea usually fetches the second highest price on international markets. To the north, Eldoret is the largest town on the Uasin Gishu highlands. The town was founded by Afrikaners from South Africa who trekked to the plateau in wagons in the 1920s. Today, wheat and timber are the principal products of the surrounding farmlands, and within the town Moi University is Kenya's newest campus.

As the B2 heads north from Eldoret towards Kitale, Kenya's second highest mountain comes into view. Measuring 80 kilometres across at its base, Mount Elgon rises to a height of 4 322 metres, its summit encircling an extinct volcanic crater. During a visit to Mount Elgon in 1883, Joseph Thomson was convinced that the mountain's caves had been excavated by humans, but it appears that elephants have been at least partly responsible for their formation. In regions of high rainfall, soils are often leached and lack minerals required by animals. Over many hundreds of years, elephants have tunnelled into the rock of the Mount Elgon caves in search of mineral-rich rock. Besides the fascinating caves, imposing forests of *Podocarpus*, juniper and Elgon olive can be explored on Elgon's lower slopes, while the summit conceals a dramatic crater and the unique plants of the Afro-alpine zone.

North of Kitale, Kenya's smallest national park, the two-square-kilometre Saiwa Swamp, was proclaimed to protect the swamp-dwelling sitatunga antelope. A few kilometres north at Kapenguria, a school room marks the site of Kenyatta's 1952 trial. Beyond Kapenguria, the road tumbles rapidly down the Cherangani Hills to the searing deserts of the north; but in western Kenya, it is ultimately Lake Victoria that beckons. On Rusinga Island, just west of Uyoma Point where Lake Victoria narrows to a width of six kilometres, one of Kenya's most respected politicians is buried. Tom Mboya was Kenyatta's right-hand man, and in the 1960s it was widely considered that he would become Kenyatta's successor until his assassination on 5 July 1969 in central Nairobi. At his birthplace on the island, and on land owned by his family, a white dome marks the site of Tom Mboya's mausoleum.

Over the rippled surface of the immense lake, late afternoon rays of coppery sunlight break through the cloud bank that broods over the far distant horizon. The light beams are refracted to strike the surface as if they were a fan of fine golden silk. Somewhere above the line where the rays are swallowed by the dark waters, pale islands shimmer as if they were mirages in the northern desert. A dozen slender fishing dhows, silhouetted now by a swathe of dancing light, await the coming of night, as they have done on these waters for so many hundreds of years.

Vast waters, sun-scorched deserts, ice-carved jagged peaks, misty forests, herds of game wandering across broad savannas and a coast of white beaches and ancient unsolved riddles — one African country has it all. Kenya is a land of contrasts, its beauty lying in its very diversity.

GATEWAY TO KENYA

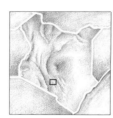

IN KENYA, ALL ROADS lead ultimately to Nairobi. For the majority of visitors arriving for a safari or a beach holiday in Kenya, Nairobi is the most likely entry portal. Functioning as Kenya's political and economic core, it is also the largest city in East Africa. Central Nairobi is a compact business district of some four square kilometres that embraces many fine hotels, modern skyscrapers, curio markets and a blend of diverse cultures. Although the city is located 140 kilometres south of the equator, its high altitude produces one of the finest climates of the world's major cities. Internationally, Nairobi exerts a significant influence and in fact two United Nations organizations operate from headquarters in the city.

Nairobi began in 1899 as a temporary railway camp set up on the edge of a malaria-infested swamp. The settlement grew rapidly and soon outstripped Mombasa as East Africa's principal town. Today, Nairobi has spread over 500 square kilometres and is home to two million people. Over the past century, the city's inhabitants have fashioned an identifiable urban culture from a composite of African, Asian and European influences. But in this often bustling city, only five kilometres separate the new Africa from the old. Nairobi National Park, on the central business district's southern edge, safeguards a valuable 117-square-kilometre expanse of grassland and forest. Lion, cheetah, leopard, black rhino and buffalo can be seen against the backdrop of the city's tall skyscrapers, a mere 20-minute drive from downtown Nairobi.

An open-air church service (left) in Uhuru Park. Nairobi's four-square-kilometre central business district lies to the west of the green swathe of the park, across the six-lane Uhuru Highway. In the compact and easily explored city centre, 15 hotels cater for visitors. The impressive Kenyatta Conference Centre, across the road from the nation's parliament, dominates central Nairobi's skyline. On a clear day the peaks of Kilimanjaro and Mount Kenya are visible from the restaurant on the 28th floor.

Modern skyscrapers (above and right) in central Nairobi provide a sharp contrast to the malaria-infested swamp that occupied the site chosen for a temporary railway storage yard in 1899, while railway engineers tried to find the best route up the steep wall of the Rift Valley. Although there was no intention of developing a capital city or a major business centre, settlers soon poured into the camp. Many of the 22 000 workmen who had been hired in India to work on the railway were accommodated on the site. From this humble and hazardous beginning, Nairobi's population grew rapidly and soon surpassed that of Mombasa. In 1950 Nairobi received city status. The city continued to expand and now covers an area exceeding 500 square kilometres and is home to two million people. As the economic and political hub of Kenya, Nairobi exerts a considerable regional and international influence. The headquarters of the United Nations' Environment and Habitat programmes are based in the city. Situated 140 kilometres south of the equator at an altitude of 1 700 metres, the city enjoys one of the finest climates in the world. Favourite tourist rendezvous points include the tudor-styled Norfolk Hotel, and the New Stanley Hotel's Thorn Tree Café, surrounding an enormous yellow-fever tree. The adjacent streets lead past curio shops, bookshops, restaurants, art galleries, museums, markets and historic buildings. Transport within central Nairobi is rapid and reliable. Visitors can choose from options that include minibus taxis, known locally as *matatus*, and genuine London cabs.

The City Market (opposite, right and above right), three blocks north of Kenyatta Avenue, is well known for its array of fruit, vegetables, flowers, baskets and curios. Although never used as such, the building housing the market was designed as an aircraft hangar in the 1930s. As the market is centrally situated, it attracts large numbers of tourists. It is an ideal starting place for any visitor who is unfamiliar with Nairobi's diverse range of fresh produce and curios. Taxi drivers are always on hand to transport the visitor back to a city centre hotel.

Nairobi's colourful *matatus* (above left) provide reliable, cheap and rapid transport for the majority of the city's inhabitants. It is estimated that one in every 15 vehicles in Kenya is a *matatu*. They are frequently overcrowded and may travel at speeds that exceed traffic regulations. The name originated from the Swahili *senti tatu*, or 'three cents', a reference to the original fare. Although fares have increased somewhat over the years, they are still very low by Western standards.

Nairobi National Park (left) lies a mere five kilometres south of Parliament, and conserves a valuable 117 square kilometres of forest and savanna. This is one place in Kenya where tourist hype is not exaggerated: it is actually possible to photograph a pride of lions within a 20-minute drive of a hotel room in the city centre. Cheetah, leopard, hyena, giraffe, zebra, buffalo, hippo and a dozen species of antelope are also present. Apart from some 50 black rhino that were re-introduced, all of the park's animals occur naturally and form part of the larger game herds of southern Kenya.

Daphne Sheldrick's conservation trust (above) is situated in a corner of the Nairobi National Park. Orphaned wild animals such as black rhino, elephant and zebra are raised until they can be rehabilitated into the wild. Daphne has devoted her life to the study of African animals and has perfected techniques for successfully raising orphaned wild animals. Author of several books on Tsavo National Park, Daphne lived through the drought of 1970 that caused the death of an estimated 9 000 elephants in the park. Daphne remains a fierce opponent of any proposal to cull elephants.

The Crowned Crane (above) is the only member of the crane family found in Kenya. It occurs on open plains, marshes and cultivated land. In flight, cranes often emit a honking call not dissimilar to the calls of a flock of geese. The Crowned Crane is a fairly common bird of the western highlands and Uganda, and is often encountered in the Saiwa Swamp National Park and in the Masai Mara National Reserve.

Buffalo (right) are frequently seen grazing the open plains of Nairobi National Park, often accompanied by flocks of white cattle egrets. Many visitors to Kenya are anxious to see the 'big five' animals. The national park contains four of these (elephant herds are missing although orphans are kept by Daphne Sheldrick), and offers excellent opportunities for viewing lion, black rhino and buffalo.

The picturesque tea plantations (left, above and right) of Limuru lie about 30 kilometres west of Nairobi, on the lip of the Rift Valley. At a brisk altitude of 2 225 metres, Limuru is ideal for tea production and produces some of Kenya's finest tea. The crop was first planted on Kiambethu Farm by Albert McDonnell in 1903. Visits to the farm, now managed by McDonnell's daughter, Mrs Evelyn Mitchell, can be arranged. Upon arrival, visitors are served tea, coffee and homemade biscuits. Mrs Mitchell then describes the history of tea farming at Limuru and conducts visitors on a tour of the estate. The visitors return to the large farmhouse for lunch, served either in the dining room or out on the lawn depending on the weather. Tea is best grown at high altitudes and in regions where rainfall is high. Although the crop is suited to large-scale plantation production, it can be grown by smallholders. An estimated 170 000 smallholders cultivate 68 000 hectares of this crop, contributing an estimated 55 per cent of Kenya's total tea production, which in good years can exceed 200 000 tons. The leaves are picked every morning by teams of pickers. Only the youngest and most tender of the leaves are picked from the bushes.

Karen Blixen's house (top). The spacious gardens surrounding Karen Blixen's house and the splendid view of the hills they afford evoke the Africa of the Danish author's writings. Her literary works still inspire journeys to Africa. The farm was sold in 1931 when the coffee crop finally failed, but the house reassuringly still contains many of her personal belongings (above) as well as several replicas made for the successful movie *Out of Africa*.

The fertile highlands bordering the Rift Valley (right), once the exclusive domain of white settlers, were subdivided after independence and are now intensively farmed in sharp contrast to the drier acacia scrub of the Rift Valley floor. Only seven per cent of the land in Kenya can be classed as high quality; much of the country receives inadequate rainfall for crop production, and demands for arable land are intense.

The interior of Hog Ranch (left and below), American writer and photographer Peter Beard's tented home. The walls are pasted with photographs, including those of the Somali model, Iman, whom Beard 'discovered' in the streets of Nairobi. Situated in the hills to the west of Nairobi, Hog Ranch is composed of a collection of tents and lean-tos on a 1 800-hectare ranch. The camp represents Beard's efforts to reproduce a retreat free from modern influence. Lighting is provided by a generator, fridges are operated by gas, and the camp does not have a telephone. Peter Beard is a divergent thinker and writer who has made Kenya his home for the past 40 years. Inspired by Karen Blixen's writings, at the age of 21 he visited her at Rungstedlung in Denmark in 1961. When Karen Blixen died a year later, she left her entire photographic collection to Beard, which includes photographs of ex-American president Theodore Roosevelt's hunting safaris, and the Duke and Prince of Wales drinking tea on the veranda of Blixen's house. After Blixen's death, Beard employed six former members of her household staff, including Blixen's cook, Kamante Gatura, and his family. Although Peter Beard has written several books, he is best known for *The End of the Game*, published in 1965. The book included old safari snapshots and photographs gleaned from Blixen's collection, and graphically illustrates the mass destruction of wildlife that took place during the twentieth century.

Traditional Kikuyu dress (above) is seldom seen today except where traditional culture is preserved for tourists, such as at the Bomas of Kenya, a traditional village 10 kilometres from the centre of Nairobi along Langata Road. Nowadays the Kikuyu are more typically represented by politicians, bankers, business leaders and farmers. The Kikuyu were prominent in early political movements, and have played an active role in Kenyan politics since the 1940s.

The Ngong Hills (right) as seen from Nairobi National Park; the hills form the eastern edge of the Rift Valley. Maasai legend would have us believe that the distinctive rounded summits of the Ngong Hills originated when a giant tripped over Kilimanjaro and fell, clutching a handful of the earth. On her farewell journey from Nairobi to Mombasa, Blixen remarked how her beloved hills were 'slowly smoothed and levelled out by the hand of distance'.

ALPINE AFRICA

THE KIKUYU CALL IT *Kirinyaga*, meaning 'white mountain' or 'place of brightness'. Africa's second tallest mountain, Mount Kenya soars above the central highlands, attaining a height of 5 199 metres at its summit. At one time the mountain was a fiery volcano, but over the ages its peaks have been carved by wind and ice, and it now resembles a rough black diamond. Positioned astride the equator, Mount Kenya's summit features glaciers and fascinating glacial characteristics. The uppermost reaches are home to the bizarre plants of the Afro-alpine zone — strange gigantic mutations of plants that are small and insignificant elsewhere in the world.

Across the central highlands and on the edge of the deep Rift Valley, volcanic eruptions produced a high plateau known as the Aberdares. A secluded preserve of mist-shrouded moors, clear rivers, and damp forests, the Aberdares became the stage for the Mau Mau uprising in the 1950s. Today, much of the Aberdares are protected within a national park. From the elevated plateau, the highest waterfalls in Kenya plunge into the forested valleys inhabited by elephant and buffalo. Apart from its scenic splendours, the Aberdares are most often associated with two well-known forest game-viewing lodges, namely Treetops and The Ark.

Between the two peaks, benefiting from the favourable climate and reliable rainfall of the highlands, almost a quarter of Kenya's people farm the fertile soil of the area. Smallholders now produce the major share of the country's export crops of tea, coffee and pyrethrum.

The upper reaches of the Teleki Valley on Mount Kenya (left) enclose some of the country's most dramatic scenery. The Naro Moru River flows down the centre of the deep ice-scoured valley that has been eroded over the millennia by glaciers. Although seven of the mountain's 18 glaciers have disappeared since John Gregory explored the peaks in 1893, Mount Kenya contains fine examples of glacial features such as U-shaped valleys, horns, and jagged aretes, or ridges.

47

Afro-alpine vegetation (above and right). Hikers on Mount Kenya's upper reaches pass through a fascinating botanical zone of Afro-alpine vegetation characterized by unique plants belonging to the genera *Lobelia* and *Senecio*. *Lobelia deckenii*, endemic to Mount Kenya, is recognized by its tall erect flower that grows to a height of seven metres. The 'ostrich plume lobelia' is a soft furry species, but the most noticeable plants are the tree groundsels (*Senecio keniodendron*), a relative of grassland forbs, that can grow to a height of 10 metres. In 1949 a 715-square-kilometre national park, coinciding roughly with the 3 200-metre contour, was established to conserve Mount Kenya, while a 2 000-square-kilometre forest reserve was proclaimed to safeguard the lower slopes. Climbers ascending the mountain along any of the three main routes pass through five distinct vegetation zones. After hiking through the dense forests of the lower slopes, a zone of giant bamboo is reached. A *Hagenia-Hypericum* forest replaces the bamboo until hikers enter a subalpine moorland of sedges and coarse tussock grasses. Above the moors, the botanical wonderland of the Afro-alpine zone awaits climbers. Many species of alpine plants, known as herbs on other high mountains, often reach astonishing heights on Mount Kenya.

The verdant forests of the high Aberdares (opposite bottom) concealed the Mau Mau – a guerrilla movement that revolted against British rule – for four years in the 1950s. The 'forest fighters', as the Mau Mau guerrillas were known, were ill-equipped and forced to rely on the dense forests for concealment. The Aberdares are now protected.

The Aberdare Country Club (opposite top) is the rendezvous point for visits to The Ark, a forest lodge situated high in the misty forests on the Aberdare slopes. A converted mansion that dates back to 1937, the club offers a variety of sports, including golf, tennis, bowls, swimming and trout fishing. Game drives on the club's game farm are an added attraction.

Fourteen Falls near Thika (above). After heavy rains have fallen on the highlands, the 27-metre-high falls on the Athi River are transformed into a roaring torrent. The falls and surroundings are a popular picnic site on weekends. The Athi River begins in the highlands near Nairobi, and then flows southeast across the plains to join the Tsavo River in dry bush country.

Coffee (left, top and above) is a crop that was originally indigenous to Ethiopia. Today, smallholders on the central highlands of Kenya produce 60 per cent of Kenya's fine arabica coffee; of the 156 000 hectares under this crop, some 118 000 hectares now being farmed by the smallholders. Since arabica coffee was introduced by missionaries in 1901, the crop has developed into one of Kenya's principal foreign exchange earners.

A flock of sheep grazing in a wheatfield (overleaf). Commercial farms occupy much of the land near Timau, on Mount Kenya's northwestern slopes. But in a country where one-tenth of the land supports about 75 per cent of the population, fertile land is understandably at a premium. In this region many peasants now farm the narrow verge between the main road and the commercial farms.

The jagged central peaks of Mount Kenya (left), encircled by mist and with glaciers clinging to the vertical crags, appear forbidding to a lone hiker. The large Tyndall Glacier straddles the gap between Point Piggott and the mist-wrapped peaks of Batian and Nelion. The Kikuyu believe that their god, Ngai, lives in the high peaks and gave the surrounding fertile highlands to Gikuyu, the first Kikuyu. Barefoot Kikuyu mystics have been known to climb the peaks.

The Mount Kenya Safari Club (above) near Nanyuki is a luxury five-star hotel once owned by Hollywood stars and oil sheiks. The club is now owned by Lonrho Hotels, and is set amidst 40 hectares of lawns, flowerbeds and ponds on the western slopes of Mount Kenya. The equator runs through the middle of the main buildings overlooking the lawns and golf course. The club is surrounded by a 500-hectare game ranch that was founded by William Holden.

The giant forest hog (above) shares the Aberdare forests with buffalo, bushbuck, bushpig, leopard and an estimated 2 800 elephant. The hog typically weighs about 135 kilograms, twice as much as the more common bushpig. The giant forest hog prefers forests interspersed with open grassy clearings. It is found on Kenya's high mountains and in riverine forests in western Kenya.

The Ark game-viewing lodge (top and right) is similar in appearance to the biblical ark. It is situated high in the Aberdare forests and accommodates 79 guests. The Ark is approached along a raised wooden walkway that leads through the forest canopy. From five different levels, guests can view a procession of animals including the chestnut-coloured bongo, giant forest hog and Sykes' monkey.

The Treetops forest lodge (above) began in 1932 as a simple tree house. It was burned down by Mau Mau fighters in 1954 and rebuilt a few years later. A plaque recalls that 'in this Mgumu tree Her Royal Highness the Princess Elizabeth succeeded to the throne', a reference to the death of the British king while Elizabeth and Prince Philip were on a visit to Kenya in 1952.

The elusive bongo (left) favours the bamboo thickets and dense forests of Kenya's highest ranges. Bongo are largely nocturnal and spend much of the day in dense thicket. While their status on Mount Kenya is uncertain, bongo are occasionally seen by visitors staying at The Ark in the Aberdares National Park. Elsewhere in Kenya, bongo occur in the Cheranganis and in the forests of the Mau Escarpment.

The misty forests of the Aberdares (opposite) contrast sharply with the neatly cultivated fields of coffee and fenced livestock paddocks of the Kikuyu smallholders. A 1 800-square-kilometre national park and surrounding forest reserve protect the higher reaches of the range, one of the finest examples of Afro-montane vegetation in Africa and one of Kenya's most picturesque parks. Vegetaton in the Aberdares is mostly affected by the altitude of the region. Dense montane rainforests cover the lower slopes up to around the 2 400-metre mark, bamboo thickets clothe the slopes up to approximately 3 000 metres, moss-wrapped hagenia forest occurs up to 3 400 metres, and above this zone the open moors stretch to the high peaks. From the town of Nyeri a track climbs through the varying vegetation zones.

The Karatina market (left and below). The town of Karatina lies in the heart of Kikuyu country. The main A2 road north across the highlands describes a wide arc encircling the lower western slopes of Mount Kenya, passing Thika, Sagana and Karatina along the route to Nyeri. The fertile volcanic soils of the highlands are intensely cultivated by Kikuyu smallholders and produce much of Kenya's fine coffee. Karatina is a bustling town that serves as an important marketplace for the smallholders from the surrounding densely populated highlands. Highland towns are typically raucous, crowded centres that overflow with people and merchandise. Compared to many African nations, Kenya has a high Gross National Product estimated at US$8 500 million in 1994. The nation's commitment to free enterprise, and the importance of business acumen, is immediately apparent in any of the highland towns. Goods and services of all descriptions and variations are traded daily in the frenetic markets. Apart from providing valuable employment opportunities, in many instances these markets more than double the space that's available for trading in the formal sector.

The equator signpost (above), situated where the main A2 road crosses the equator, about two kilometres south of Nanyuki. Curio sellers have erected stalls to attract motorists stopping at the signpost. Nanyuki grew rapidly after the railway reached the town in the 1920s. Settler's Store, located on the main road, has been trading since 1938. Kenya's largest airforce base is situated nearby, and the district is used to train British soldiers.

Thomson's Falls (right) on the Ewaso Narok River at the town of Nyahururu. The 73-metre-high falls and the comfort of the adjacent Thomson's Falls Lodge – a cosy hotel that was built in 1931 and has the atmosphere of a highland farmhouse – make it a popular stopover for tourists travelling between Buffalo Springs and Samburu national reserves and the Rift Valley lakes. The town is the highest in Kenya.

GREAT RIFT VALLEY

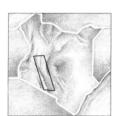

THE RIFT VALLEY CARVES a 6 000-kilometre trench down the middle of Africa. This 50- to 90-kilometre-wide rent in the earth's crust is visible from a spacecraft 150 000 kilometres out in space. Dormant volcanoes rise above the flat floor of the valley, and a chain of lakes has formed in the depressions. The most well known of these lakes is Nakuru, one of the finest bird-watching destinations in the world. Lesser flamingos, numbering as many as 1.5 million, often stain the lake's shores pink with their amassed plumage. Some 60 kilometres north, Lake Bogoria has been called the most beautiful scene in Africa. Hot springs, dry acacia woodland, a flamingo-crowded lake, and the eastern wall of the Rift Valley rising 630 metres above the lake confirm this description.

One of only two freshwater lakes in Kenya's Rift Valley, Lake Baringo is the largest of the central lakes, while the source of its freshwater inflow remains a mystery. The lake is a bird-watching paradise and 450 species have been identified. Hippo and crocodile are also present. Small in number, the Njemps tribe fishes the lake from lightweight canoes.

Within easy reach of Nairobi, Lake Naivasha was once the retreat of the self-indulgent settlers of *White Mischief* fame. Today it is better known for its enormous flower estates, its fever-tree-lined shores, Africa's only geothermal power station, and Joy Adamson's perfectly situated house, Elsamere, now run as a conservation centre. Lake Naivasha is a popular weekend boating venue and bird-watching retreat. The surrounding high walls of the Rift Valley and Mau Escarpment further enhance the magnificent setting.

The Great Rift Valley (left) is one of Kenya's most dramatic geographical features and includes nine dormant volcanoes and seven lakes. In 1893 John Gregory conducted the first exploration of the Rift Valley by a geologist. Gregory predicted that the trough – ranging in width from 50 to 90 kilometres – that runs for 6 000 kilometres down the length of Africa would be visible from the moon. Photographs taken of the earth from 150 000 kilometres out in space confirm the accuracy of Gregory's prediction.

Lake Magadi (above, opposite top and opposite bottom) is situated on the floor of the Rift Valley and is the most southerly of Kenya's lakes. At an altitude of 579 metres, Lake Magadi is one of the hottest places in the country. The lake consists of a vast shallow pool of alkaline water and soda. Subterranean springs in the lake bed produce vast quantities of sodium chloride (table salt), and sodium carbonate (soda ash) coloured pink by algae. In the intense heat of the Rift Valley floor, salt crystals form on top of the soda. A company town, built by the Magadi Soda Company on a peninsula that juts out into the lake, accommodates the workers who extract the soda. Soda ash is Kenya's principal mineral export and Lake Magadi is the second largest source of soda in the world. Once extracted, the soda is loaded onto railway cars and railed to the coast for export. About 240 000 tons of soda ash are extracted from the lake bed. Apart from the lake's fascinating soda fields, Magadi is popular among bird-watchers.

Hell's Gate National Park (opposite), just south of Lake Naivasha, is thought to have been an ancient outlet for the lake. Apart from the rugged scenery of the gorge, the national park includes Fischer's Tower, a lone 25-metre-high volcanic plug. Another lone rock tower, Ol Basta, indicates the half-way mark of the 24-kilometre hike through the spectacular gorge.

Pelicans at Lake Naivasha (left). Volcanic activity in the Rift Valley has given rise to a chain of lakes, several volcanoes and dramatic scenery within easy reach of Nairobi. Lake Naivasha is the closest body of water to the city.

A Nubian Woodpecker (above) at Lake Baringo. This woodpecker prefers habitats such as open bush and acacia woodland, both of which can be found around Lake Baringo. The lake is renowned for its bird-watching and a staggering 450 species of birds have been recorded. The resident birds at Lake Baringo are either permanent or migrant, having flown to the area to escape the European winter. As well as the Nubian Woodpecker, the Grey-headed Bush Shrike and the Violet Wood Hoopoe have been seen near the lake. The world record for the number of bird species recorded in 24 hours was set at Lake Baringo.

Greater Flamingos (above) and Sacred Ibis (opposite top), common residents of marshes, swampland, rivers and lakes, on the waters of Lake Naivasha. About four million Lesser Flamingos and 45 000 Greater Flamingos inhabit the Rift lakes. Greater Flamingos feed on small invertebrates and crustacea. Both species of flamingo feed by drawing water into their bills; the food is trapped by fine laminae that line the bill.

Lake Naivasha (right), at an altitude of 1 908 metres, is the highest of Kenya's Rift Valley lakes, and the second largest. Flanked by the Mau Escarpment to the west and the high Aberdares to the east, Lake Naivasha is beautifully situated and has become a popular weekend venue for water sports. Travellers can stay in two hotels on the southern shore, and Joy Adamson's former house Elsamere is now run as a conservation centre.

Lake Bogoria (above and right) was described by the nineteenth-century explorer, John Gregory, as 'the most beautiful sight in all Africa'. The eastern wall of the Rift Valley rises 630 metres above the narrow, alkaline lake which is about 60 kilometres north of Lake Nakuru. The lake is renowned for its enormous flocks of Lesser Flamingos and the hot springs and geysers that erupt on its western shore. A national reserve protects 107 square kilometres of the surrounding dry woodland, and has the reputation of being the best location in Kenya for sightings of greater kudu. Other animals that can be seen include plains zebra, impala, dik-dik and Grant's gazelle. Several campsites provide relief from the heat.

Njemps gourds (left), used for carrying milk, are decorated with attractive etchings typical of those found on Maasai gourds. Although they have abandoned some of the Maasai cultural traits, the Njemps dress and decorate themselves similarly to the Maasai.

Rothschild's giraffe (opposite) in the Lake Nakuru National Park. This particular species is named after Lionel Rothschild, a hunter who, in the 1880s, described a group of unusually marked animals from western Kenya. The giraffe dwindled in number until they were confined to a ranch near Soy in western Kenya. In 1978 a herd of 26 giraffes was moved to the safety of the Lake Nakuru park where their population has rapidly increased.

The Njemps people (above) of Lake Baringo in the Great Rift Valley have abandoned their previously nomadic lifestyle and now fish Lake Baringo's waters from their small canoes. These fishing vessels are in fact similar to the coracles used by fishermen in Europe thousands of years ago. In the past the region in which the Njemps people now live formed part of Maasai territory. As the Maasai people and their cattle migrated southwards, a small group remained behind and abandoned their pastoral lifestyle. The Njemps build their small canoes from the wood of the ambach tree. Although they own cattle and goats, the rugged and inhospitable floor of the Rift Valley has forced the Njemps to depend primarily on fishing.

The Pokot people of western Kenya (above left, above right and opposite) share many cultural traits with the Turkana of the northwestern deserts, although they belong to the Kalenjin grouping. Pokot women typically wear decorative necklaces and earrings made from metal and beads. Warriors wear the headdress of painted clay that is a feature of the Turkana. The tribe occupies a territory that forms a broad arc from Lake Baringo to the Ugandan border. The Pokot of the dry woodland of the Kerio Valley, bordered by the dramatic Elgeyo Escarpment to the west, are strict pastoralists. Some of the Pokot of the lowlands have become skilled gold-panners, and still manage to find gold in the Nasolot River. Those who live in the fertile Cherangani Hills are known as the Masopot, or 'mountain dwellers'. The hill Pokot grow maize, millet and tobacco, and keep herds of livestock. Over the centuries, this tribe has developed sophisticated methods for irrigating crops. Crafts such as pottery and metalwork are practised by the hill Pokot. It is thought that the Pokot were originally agriculturists and adapted pastoralism in arid regions where crop farming was impractical.

ON SAFARI

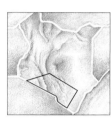

THE WORD 'SAFARI' – 'to journey' in Swahili – has become synonymous with a visit to Kenya's world-renowned national parks and reserves. On the endless acacia-dotted savannas of southern Kenya, wildlife spectacles of bygone ages are still enacted each year. Southern Kenya is home to the Maasai people, a dignified group of once-nomadic pastoralists who shepherd large herds of cattle and goats across the plains. The Maasai respect wildlife and it was not by accident that Kenya's major wildlife parks were established on Maasailand. The major share of Kenya's 1.5 million wild animals inhabits this region.

Amboseli is one of the most popular of Kenya's national reserves. Below the awe-inspiring summit of Mount Kilimanjaro, elephant and buffalo feed in swamps created by water flowing from the mountain's higher slopes. Amboseli is the epitome of what one expects from an African safari and the juxtaposition of Kilimanjaro's imposing heights, dry savanna and verdant swamplands guarantees its continuing popularity.

West across the Rift Valley, the Masai Mara National Reserve attracts 700 000 wildebeest each July from the neighbouring Serengeti. Even when the migration has passed, the reserve's fertile volcanic soils still support on average 340 000 head of game. Lion, cheetah, hyena and elephant are abundant and over 153 000 people visit the reserve each year to experience its natural wonders.

On the semi-arid plains to the east of Amboseli, the Tsavo National Park conserves a wildlife reserve larger in area than Wales or Massachusetts. Eight game lodges, most of them positioned overlooking extensive plains or mountainous terrain, provide comfort in the midst of this untrammelled wilderness.

Game-viewing in the Masai Mara National Reserve (left). The open grasslands of the Mara's plains support enormous herds of game, and the highest concentration of lions in Africa. Over the past two decades, tourist camps have mushroomed in response to the Mara's rising reputation as one of the finest parks in Africa. Lodges and tented camps can now provide over 1 000 beds in 19 separate establishments for the 150 000 visitors that visit the Mara each year.

A lioness (left) rests in a fig tree in riverine forest bordering the Mara River. In response to increasing hunting pressure, a triangle of land bounded by the Siria Escarpment, Mara River and Tanzanian border was declared a wildlife sanctuary in 1948. But hunting continued in the region, and by 1961 hunters had reduced lion numbers to nine. In response to calls for action, an area of some i 800 square kilometres was gazetted as the Masai Mara National Reserve.

The White-backed Vulture (above) is the most common of the six vulture species that occur in the Masai Mara. In flight, the White-backed Vulture is recognized by its conspicuous white rump and the white edge to its wings. The large vulture population is sustained, in part, by the activities of the Mara's many predators. Although vultures keep a safe distance at lion and hyena kills, they frequently drive the more timid cheetah from its kills.

The striking Yellow-billed Stork (left) is an uncommon bird found along the edges of rivers, floodplains and marshes. Male and female storks are similar in appearance, but the female can be distinguished by a yellow ring that encircles the eyes. Storks, either singly or in pairs, are encountered hunting for prey in the shallows of rivers or lakes.

Governors' Camp (top), a luxury tented camp established in a forest clearing near the Mara River, was a popular camping site for the governor of the 1950s, Sir Evelyn Baring. Governors' is one of the Mara's three original camps that existed prior to the tourism boom that followed the closing of the Tanzanian border in 1977. Eight of the total of 19 camps, including Governors', are located within the reserve's unfenced borders. The majority is situated along the banks of the Mara River, upstream of the reserve boundary.

Plains or Grant's zebra (right) are the first animals to migrate into the Mara from the Serengeti in Tanzania at the start of the migration cycle. The zebra herds arrive in June and return to the Serengeti in October. During the migration, the population of zebra in the Mara can increase from 65 000 in May to nearly 110 000 in June.

A mixed herd (above) of topi, plains zebra and Thomson's gazelle feed on the nourishing grasses of the Masai Mara. The open plains of the Mara support an astonishing 26 herbivore species, compared to 11 species throughout the entire continent of North America. From a combination of high rainfall, low evaporation and fertile volcanic-derived soils, the *Themeda triandra* grasslands of the Mara are capable of sustaining, on average, 340 000 wild animals, or 143 animals per square kilometre.

An olive baboon (top) occupies a prominent position, ever on the lookout for possible danger. Baboons explore the open plains, rocky hills and riverine forest. When the troop rests or feeds, the females and young occupy the centre, while the less dominant males keep watch for predators.

A mother cheetah and her three near-adult cubs (right). The open grasslands of the Mara are ideal habitat for cheetah, which may be solitary, or form small units such as this one.

A herd of elephants (above) treks through the Siana hills on the eastern boundary of the Mara. In the past, elephants were rare in the region and only 60 were recorded by Bernhard Grzimek in a 1958 survey of the neighbouring Serengeti. After the rinderpest epidemic of the 1890s that decimated cattle and game herds in the Mara region, woodlands and thickets spread rapidly. But in recent years, as elephants have increased, the thickets have given way to open plains.

The Mara River (left) viewed from the air. The river is bordered by a corridor of riverine forest and meanders across extensive plains. Riverine vegetation is the least represented habitat in the Mara and in recent decades, has begun to retreat under the combined onslaught of increasing elephants and grassland fires.

Hot-air ballooning over the Mara (right), a popular although expensive way of surveying the reserve. The idea originated in 1962 when Anthony Smith, Douglas Botting and Charl Pauw, assisted by wildlife film-maker Alan Root, flew in a balloon from Zanzibar to Serengeti.

During the annual migration (top, above and right), the Mara supports up to one million additional animals – mostly wildebeest and zebra – drawn from the Serengeti Plain in search of grazing and water. The migration is a relatively recent phenomenon that dates back to about 1969. In the 1890s the rinderpest epidemic eliminated 95 per cent of the wildebeest and cattle in the region. Veterinarians inoculated the Maasai's cattle against rinderpest, and the disease disappeared from the area. As a result, the wildebeest increased from 263 000, in 1961 further expanding to the present population of 1.4 million. The growing herds were forced to travel further north across the Serengeti Plain in their search for water and grazing, and the Mara now provides valuable dry-season grazing. Herds of zebra precede the wildebeest migration by about two to three weeks. Zebra prefer the coarser terminal section of the red oat grass (*Themeda triandra*) that is abundant in the Mara, while wildebeest prefer shorter grasses. The sight of zebra herds gathering on the banks of the Mara River is a definite sign that the enormous herds of wildebeest are not far behind.

A Maasai man (opposite) displays the attire characteristic of this proud group of pastoralists. The majority of the Maasai still adhere to their age-old traditions. In Maasai society, men undergo four complex 'rites of passage' that mark the transition from one stage of life to the next. During the *eunoto* (coming of age) ceremony young warriors, or *morani*, graduate to become junior elders. This ceremony involves many traditional rites and is the most elaborate of the Maasai's rituals. Wealth and status in Maasai society are based on cattle ownership, and their language includes dozens of names for variations in cattle coloration or pattern. Like their relatives of the northern desert, the Samburu, the Maasai dress predominantly in red.

A Maasai elder and two women (above) outside one of the huts that comprise an *enkang* – a settlement consisting of several dwellings that are constructed from branches and covered with dung. A barrier of thorn branches surrounds the settlement, and cattle are kept inside the thorny enclosure at night. Often a young calf will be kept in a corner of the dwelling for protection.

The Maasai people (overleaf) share the 40 000 square kilometres of acacia savanna in southern Kenya with large herds of cattle and game. The Maasai have always tolerated wildlife and in the past hunted buffalo and eland only during times of drought. Two of Kenya's most important wildlife reserves – Masai Mara and Amboseli – are situated on Maasailand.

Masai giraffe (left) provide a colourful complement to the awe-inspiring backdrop of ice-capped Kilimanjaro. Similar images have illustrated countless articles and books on African wildlife. Several of Hollywood's African adventure movies have been filmed on location at Amboseli. The cabins at Ol Tukai, now rented out by the Kajiado district council, were built as part of the set for the 1948 movie *The Snows of Kilimanjaro*.

Amboseli Lodge (above) at Ol Tukai, is one of the three game lodges within the national park that caters for visitors. Kilimanjaro Safari Lodge is also located in the vicinity, and Amboseli Serena Lodge adjoins the Enkongo Narok swamp, a few kilometres to the south. Of Kenya's major national parks and reserves, Amboseli is closest to Nairobi. While many visitors arrive on fly-in safaris, the journey by road from Nairobi is mostly on a tarred surface.

The clear waters of Mzima Springs
(left) in Tsavo West sustain a
fever-tree-lined oasis inhabited by
hippo (above), crocodile, waterbirds
and fish. From an underwater hide,
visitors enjoy a rare opportunity of
viewing life below the surface of the
pools. The water that gushes out of
the ground, at an estimated
250 million litres a day, originates in
the volcanic Chyulu Hills 25 kilometres
to the north.

The Shetani lava flow (right)
(shetani means 'devil' in Kiswahili) is
evidence of volcanic activity that took
place in Tsavo within the last 200
years. In the distance, behind the black
lava, the lava cones forming the
Chyulu Hills filter rainwater that later
re-emerges at Mzima Springs.

The Masai giraffe (left) occurs south of the Tana River on the acacia savannas of southern Kenya. This species of giraffe is easily identified by its irregular reddish-brown spots and ochre-coloured skin. It frequents lightly wooded savannas and open woodlands. The changes in the vegetation of Tsavo from dense thicket to open woodland have favoured this giraffe and the population is estimated at 3 600 animals.

Tsavo East National Park (top) is an immense 11 747-square-kilometre wilderness bisected by the Galana River. Although much of the region receives a low annual rainfall, nearly 400 species of birds and 40 large mammal species occur. Prior to 1989, poachers were killing an average of three elephants a day in Tsavo. Following a military-style crackdown on poaching, the park lost only 20 elephants to poachers over a five-year period from 1990 to 1994.

The yellow baboon (above) differs from the olive baboon of western Kenya – it is a slender animal with a yellow-fawn back and white underside. The yellow baboon is similar in appearance to the chacma baboon.

Verreaux's Eagle Owl (above left), also known as the Giant Eagle Owl, is nocturnal. The riverine vegetation bordering the Galana and Voi rivers in Tsavo East is its ideal habitat.

The shy lesser kudu (above) favours dense thorn bush and shrub, particularly in dry areas. Before the rapid increase in elephant numbers that occurred in the 1960s, lesser kudu were more common in Tsavo. Although this antelope is locally common, the total population in Tsavo is not large and has been estimated at about 2 000.

Lugard's Falls (right), on the Galana River in Tsavo East, exhibit intriguing rock patterns. The falls were named after Britain's first proconsul in East Africa, Captain Lugard. Where the river is channelled through a narrow neck, it is possible to stand with one foot on either bank, watched by the crocodiles in the pools below.

The Vulturine Guineafowl (right) inhabits dry thornbush and semi-arid country in eastern Kenya. As the head appears small for a bird of its size, it has been likened to a vulture. In reality this guineafowl is unrelated to both vultures and the common Helmeted Guineafowl. Vulturine Guineafowl are gregarious birds.

A view of the waterhole at Voi (left). From the vantage point of Voi Safari Lodge's elevated position, visitors can track large herds of buffalo approaching the waterholes at the base of the hill on which the lodge stands. Buffalo herds are often present, together with elephant, which are increasing again in number following years of rampant poaching.

The Voi Safari Lodge (top), built on the crest of a rocky hill, overlooks the vastness of Tsavo East, and is renowned for its commanding views over the wilderness. The lodge is located within easy reach of the main Nairobi to Mombasa road. The southern third of the park south of the Galana River is accessible to visitors, while much of the remainder consists of a barren and uncharted wilderness.

THE CORAL COAST

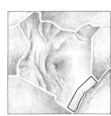

THE KENYAN COASTLINE STRETCHES for 700 kilometres from Wasini Island near Tanzania to the Kiunga Marine Reserve on the border with Somalia. Along this route, the coastline digresses through drowned river valleys, mangrove swamps, river deltas, coral reefs and mysterious islands. Since the mid-1970s, the coral coast has become Kenya's premier tourist retreat. Arguably the finest beachside haven in Africa, over 50 hotels and numerous clubs and cottages cater for tourists.

Much of the coral coast's appeal stems from the coral reefs that stretch from Wasini Island in the south to north of Malindi. Protected from powerful waves, except at river mouths where fresh water prevents the growth of coral, the coast is characterized by smooth white beaches of coral sand. Groves of coconut palms, sheltered bays of turquoise-coloured tropical sea, and schools of multicoloured fish complement a near-perfect setting. But apart from the coral coast's many idyllic beaches, underwater wonders and coral reefs, an air of mystery is lent to the sublime setting by puzzling ruins of Swahili settlements dating back to the eighth century, uncharted mangrove swamps, and remote islands.

The Kenyan coast, for convenience, can be divided into three sections: the south coast from Mombasa to Shimoni; the north coast from Mombasa to Malindi; and the remote north including the Tana River mouth and the islands of Lamu, Manda and Pate. The most popular tourist beaches are found along the coastal strip stretching 90 kilometres south of Mombasa that includes the popular resorts of Tiwi and Diani beaches. The northern resorts of Nyali, Bamburi, Shanzu and Watamu are accessible from the coastal road that ends at the ancient town of Malindi, where the Portuguese mariner, Vasco da Gama, erected a stone cross in 1499. Adventurous travellers may wish to attempt the journey north to the island town of Lamu, a Swahili port that has remained largely unaffected by the modern age.

The Kenyan coast (left) is shielded from the destructive action of waves by offshore coral reefs for over half of its 700-kilometre length, from Vanga on the Tanzanian border to the remote Kiunga Marine Reserve bordering Somalia. Arguably the finest coastal area in Africa, since the mid-1970s the coastal strip has become one of Kenya's prime tourist destinations.

The Friday mosque (right) dominates the village of Shela, a few kilometres south of Lamu. The mosque was built in 1829, and its rocket-shaped minaret, not usually seen on mosques in East Africa, has attracted much interest. A narrow channel separates Shela from Manda Island, known for its mysterious ruined towns of Takwa and Manda. Takwa was a thriving centre until it was mysteriously abandoned in the seventeenth century.

The streets of Lamu (below right) bear witness to the Omani and Hadhrami Arab influence of the late nineteenth century in the buildings that line the town's narrow lanes and alleys. Lamu Island, measuring 12 kilometres in length and five kilometres in width, and located on Kenya's remote northern coast, has been settled for hundreds of years. The town borders the channel that separates the island from Manda, and was a thriving port in the fourteenth century, but it is likely that the site was established much earlier. Pwani Mosque, built in 1370, is one of the oldest buildings in Lamu. The fort adjacent to the mosque was built by the Omanis in 1821.

Lamu's waterfront (opposite) is its centre of attraction with the trading dhows moored along the sea wall. Lamu is an unhurried Islamic town. A maze of streets and narrow alleys crisscrosses the town revealing carved wooden doors, decorated portals and balconies, protruding fretwork balconies, and moulded plasterwork. About 30 guest houses and lodgings within the town centre encourage visitors to absorb the town's ambience. The intimate Peponi and Island hotels, three kilometres south in the village of Shela, offer superb and reasonably priced accommodation.

Door carving (left and opposite) is an ancient art that is still practised in Lamu. In the eighth and ninth centuries Arabs settled along the Kenyan coast. Offshore islands, such as Lamu and the adjacent island of Manda, were favoured settlement sites as they offered security against possible attacks from mainland tribes. Intermarriage with the local Africans took place and within a few generations the Swahili people and the Kiswahili language had arisen. Arab influence on Swahili culture is apparent in its architecture, pottery and predominantly Islamic religion, while an African influence is evident in the Kiswahili language.

A Bajun woman and grandchild
(above). The Bajun live on the islands
of the Lamu archipelago and the
coastal strip of Kenya's far northern
coast. They share a common language,
Kiswahili, with the Swahili and
Shirazi people.

Mangoes (left) are transported in
canoes down the muddy channel of
the Tana River which is Kenya's largest
river and flows eastwards across dry
bush country from its central
highland sources on Mount Kenya
and the Aberdares.

Trading dhows (right) at Lamu. Strong
trade links have existed between
Lamu and other maritime nations
for centuries.

A fisherman (above) returns with the day's catch at Malindi. Fishermen off-load their catches on the beach near the town's pier. The fish are then taken to sheds to be cleaned, and, later, to be served by the many restaurants that cater for tourists. Malindi is a popular beach resort and attracts thousands of European tourists, particularly from Germany and Italy. Tourist hotels, cottages and beach-side clubs now line the beaches to the north and south of the town's ancient centre.

Fishing dhows (right) lie beached on Malindi's protective outer reef. Malindi has been in existence for many hundreds of years. In 1498 the Portuguese mariner, Vasco da Gama, visited Malindi. The port towns of Mombasa and Malindi were bitter enemies at the time and, as da Gama had received a cool reception in Mombasa, he was almost guaranteed a warm welcome from the sultan of Malindi. Sure enough, the sultan celebrated his arrival with festivities.

The Gedi Ruins (opposite top) are among the many ruins of Swahili settlements along the Kenyan coast. Gedi was established on a site several kilometres inland from the sea. The town was typical of a medieval town in its layout – the central palace and six mosques were surrounded by two walls, beyond which the majority of Gedi's estimated 2 500 inhabitants lived. Strangely, it was unknown to the Portuguese in Malindi, a mere 15 kilometres north.

The Jumba la Mtwana Ruins (opposite bottom), across Mtwapa Creek, are all that remain of a once wealthy fourteenth-century Swahili community. The ruins are located three kilometres down a track from the main north coast road. Jumba la Mtwana is set in a grove of baobab trees, immediately above an open stretch of beach. The settlement once included four mosques of which the Mosque by the Sea was the finest. A short walk inland, the House of Many Doors appears to have been a fifteenth-century inn.

At the Juma, or Friday, Mosque (left) in Malindi, a pillar tomb built in the fifteenth century honours Sheikh Abdul Hassan. A shorter pillar tomb is thought to have been built in the nineteenth century. Pillar tombs are unique to the coast and can be found in many of the ruined settlements. At the spot where the mosque now stands, slaves were once auctioned every week until slavery was outlawed in 1873.

An aerial view of Mombasa (overleaf). The city is Kenya's second largest and East Africa's chief port and entrepôt. The island, surrounded by extensive coves and channels, provided an ideal site for the city's earliest inhabitants. Isolated from attack from the mainland, and with trade routes secured across the sea, Mombasa was a thriving port at the time of the visit in 1498 by a Portuguese fleet captained by Vasco da Gama.

Cannonballs in Fort Jesus (above). After receiving a hostile reception from the citizens of Mombasa in 1498 the Portuguese returned in 1505 and raided the city's treasure vaults. The Portuguese attacked Mombasa again in 1528 and 1589. Finally in 1593 the city was defeated by the Portuguese who began construction of the impressive Fort Jesus, overlooking the dhow harbour. The imposing fortress was designed by Giovanni Cairato, and is a fine example of fifteenth-century architecture. Commanding the headland above the old dhow harbour, Fort Jesus is Mombasa's most prominent historic building.

Fort Jesus (right). Although the Portuguese finally defeated Mombasa after nearly a century of conflict, peace did not come easily. Despite the fortress's 15-metre-high walls, it was constantly attacked. In 1696 Omani Arabs laid siege to the fortress for three years. After the citizens of Mombasa rebelled against their new Arab rulers, the Portuguese returned for a brief sojourn but were soon expelled, and they sailed from the city for the last time in 1728. Mombasa subsequently remained under Omani control until 1895 when Britain took over control of the coast until Kenyan independence in December 1963.

Mosques and minarets (opposite top and above) dominate the skyline of Mombasa's Old Town, the coastal city's leading tourist attraction. Its labyrinth of winding lanes evokes scenes reminiscent of Sindbad, the sailor from the *Arabian Nights*. Hawkers sell coconut milk on street corners, or struggle with carts loaded with merchandise. The mix of diverse peoples and cultures (opposite bottom), aromas of exotic spices and Swahili cuisine, the strong smell of *kahawa* coffee poured from copper pots, the muezzins' call to prayer, and the intense heat and humidity reinforce the ambience of the Old Town.

Mombasa has survived numerous wars and periods of occupation by foreign forces; in part, the city's sluggish pace is derived from its enduring qualities – the city has outlived all its conquerors. Located along Mbaraki Road, Mandhry Mosque, built in 1570, is Mombasa's oldest building.

Government Square is reached at the top of the stairs ascending from the dhow harbour. The square contains the Customs House, fish market and shops trading carpets, brass and chests imported from the Persian Gulf. Other shops trade in spices or fabric. Ancient tombs are found along the seafront.

The Serena Beach Hotel (left and above), located on Shanzu Beach 18 kilometres north of Mombasa, has the reputation of being one of the finest hotels in Kenya. It is the only hotel in the country that is listed as a 'Leading Hotel of the World'. The hotel's 166 air-conditioned rooms have been designed to replicate a Swahili coastal settlement. Palm-lined pathways lead past fountains and tropical gardens through the white-walled village. In recent years Kenya's coastal strip has risen in importance as a tourist retreat. The coast's diverse attractions include bays of turquoise water guarded by coral reefs, beaches of smooth white sand and swaying coconut palms, and nearly two thousand years of settlement history. Guests staying at the Serena Beach Hotel can choose from an array of coastal pleasures that include superb cuisine ranging from Italian to African, swimming, boardsailing, scuba diving and deep-sea fishing. The nearby coral gardens of the marine park can be explored in glass-bottomed boats.

The red starfish (left). Not only does the reef provide a habitat and protection for numerous diverse species of fish, but many marine animals such as the parrot fish and starfish feed on live coral. Starfish can regenerate severed limbs.

Caesio xanthonotus (opposite centre) is one of a multitude of colourful fish awaiting the scuba diver below the waves. The warm currents that wash Kenya's coastline have encouraged the growth of coral and the formation of reefs.

Dolphins (opposite top) delight tourists on a boat off the protective coral reef. Schools of dolphins often swim alongside boats, leaping into the air. Dolphins are mammals, and have acute senses of sight, hearing and taste.

Scuba divers (above) prepare to venture into the intriguing underwater world that waits to be explored off Watamu. The north coast village is a popular destination for scuba diving, snorkelling and deep-sea fishing.

A hawker (top) sells colourful garments at Jadini Beach. The concentration of tourist hotels along Kenya's beaches has encouraged an entrepreneurial boom.

Colourful houses (above) line the track that leads to Tiwi Beach. This is the first of the south coast's many fine coastal retreats. As the beach is situated about 15 kilometres south of the Likoni ferry crossing that connects Mombasa Island with the mainland, it has become popular with travellers.

Diani Beach (right), the coral coast's most popular beach-side resort, is protected by an offshore reef. Even at low tide, the water within the sanctuary formed by the offshore reef is deep enough for swimming and snorkelling among shoals of colourful tropical fish. Diani Beach's pristine shore stretches for over 10 kilometres from the mouth of the Tiwi River. As Kenya's most popular beach, the enticing pure white sands and turquoise sea have encouraged developers – over a dozen hotels line this stretch of coast.

Sisal plants (left) grow in straight rows between giant baobabs, sole remnants of the former coastal vegetation. Kenya is the third largest producer of sisal in the world; plants were introduced to Kenya from Mexico in 1908.

The majestic sable antelope (above) is protected in the Shimba Hills. The reserve safeguards Kenya's sole sable population, estimated at about 120. Although it cannot be considered common, the sable antelope is widely distributed in tropical woodland in southern and central Africa.

The tropical coastal forests (top) of the Shimba Hills National Reserve, interspersed with tall doum palms, are a marked contrast to the crowded streets of Mombasa. The reserve lies 30 kilometres south of the city's centre and preserves a valuable 196-square-kilometre tract of rolling grasslands and forest. A short 20-minute drive from the tropical heat and dampening humidity of the coast leads inland to the breezy hills, set 448 metres above sea level. One of Kenya's finest forest lodges, Shimba, is tucked into a clearing in the forest.

The impressive Kongo Mosque (opposite top) stands in the midst of a grove of giant baobabs at the mouth of the Tiwi River. The mosque is named after the Kongo Forest, and is thought to date back to the fifteenth century. Researchers believe that a Shirazi settlement occupied the site.

Coconut palms (opposite bottom) were introduced from Indonesia centuries before Portuguese explorers reached the coast. These palms now line the coast forming a distinct corridor that is visible from elevated viewpoints such as those existing in the Shimba Hills National Reserve.

Mangrove poles and a dhow (above) on Funzi Island near the popular fishing destination of Shimoni. Funzi Island is separated from the mainland of Kenya by a narrow channel that can be crossed when the tide is out. Funzi Village is located on the south side of the island. Mangrove poles such as these are transported from the extensive mangrove swamps of the coast all the way to markets in the Persian Gulf. The Kenyan government controls the cutting of mangrove trees in an effort to attempt to prevent overexploitation of what is an important resource for the country.

THE ARID NORTH

THE RUGGED MOUNTAINS and parched plains of Kenya's arid north comprise nearly three-quarters of the country. In this barren region, where rainfall rarely exceeds 500 millimetres while evaporation can exceed as much as 2 600 millimetres, small bands of hardy pastoralists struggle to survive. Once known as the Northern Frontier District, or NFD, the arid north still retains its frontier ambience. The dusty, single-street towns are connected by sandy roads that cross the arid and desolate plains dotted with stunted acacia bushes.

In the heart of this region, the sea-green waters of Lake Turkana appear like a mirage. The largest desert lake in the world, Turkana is fed by rivers flowing off the Ethiopian highlands. Located on the floor of the Rift Valley, the lake has no access to the sea, but the presence of the Nile perch suggests an ancient link with the Nile. With no outlet to the sea, dissolved salts carried into Lake Turkana by rivers and volcanic eruptions have caused its waters to become alkaline, very similar in taste to that of bottled soda water. In the inhospitable wasteland on the lake's western shore, 975 kilometres from Nairobi, Jomo Kenyatta and his fellow detainees were held between 1952 and 1959. At Loiyangalani, Kenya's smallest tribe, the el-Molo, lives in a village of palm-frond huts set on a bleak lava plain. In their bleak setting, the el-Molo, numbering about 500 people, depend on fishing for their livelihood and occasionally hunt crocodile and hippo.

East of the lake, the cool forests of the Marsabit volcano are an anachronism in this parched territory. Marsabit traps evaporation from the surrounding hot desert, converting it into moisture that sustains the dense forest and crater lakes.

Camel caravans (left) still cross Kenya's arid north. In the past, this region was known as the Northern Frontier District, or NFD, and was seen as a land of adventure, hardship and danger, a reputation that was fuelled for several years by Shifta rebels from Somalia. The barren north is a region of erratic rainfall and extreme temperatures. Its inhabitants belong largely to the Cushitic groups that inhabit Ethiopia and Somalia. These nomadic pastoralists rely on an estimated 800 000 camels for transport and for milk.

Vegetation (right and opposite) in the north consists predominantly of scattered acacia and commiphora bushes. A sparse covering of grass sometimes grows between the bushes, but during periods of prolonged drought grass may be absent for years. An estimated 72 per cent of Kenya receives less than 500 millimetres of rain per annum; evaporation in this region can exceed 2 600 millimetres. In some areas of this barren zone rainfall is often limited to less than 300 millimetres. Near Lake Turkana, volcanic activity has produced a wasteland of black lava rocks.

A Gabbra woman (below right) from Kenya's remote northern desert. The Gabbra inhabit the arid lands that stretch northwards from Mount Marsabit to the Ethiopian border including the inhospitable Dida Galgalu, the 'Plains of Darkness'. The Gabbra number fewer than 40 000 people and have survived centuries of hardship and drought. Camels are used to transport their portable homes, consisting of a bundle of curved sticks and a few mats, across the unrelenting wasteland. Viewed from a distance, the caravan of camels, each animal with the forward curve of the sticks protruding above its load, resembles a fleet of ships sailing in a desert mirage. At the edge of Gabbra territory, on the shores of Lake Turkana, fossil discoveries by Richard Leakey at Koobi Fora have confirmed that humans have been living in this region for eons.

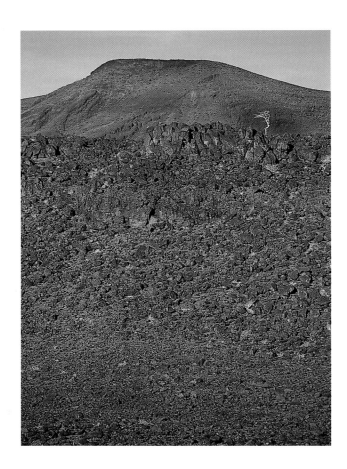

Lake Turkana (above) is sometimes called the 'Jade Sea' which is a reference to the lake's salty waters that appear to be marine-green from a distance. The world's largest desert lake, Turkana covers a vast area of 6 400 square kilometres. Although Lake Turkana has no access to the sea, the presence of the Nile perch is evidence that an ancient link with the Nile River must have once existed. The alkalinity caused by salts carried into the lake by rivers is not too high to support any life: fish, birds and crocodiles occur.

A child of the el-Molo tribe (opposite). Inhabiting a single village of palm-frond huts on Lake Turkana's desolate eastern shore, the el-Molo depend solely on fishing, and the occasional hunting of crocodile and hippo. The el-Molo (about 500 people) are thought to have migrated to the lake shore about 2 000 years ago. The words 'el-Molo' are derived from the Samburu *loo molo onsikirri*, 'the people who eat fish'. It is thought that the tribe was possibly forced to catch fish after drought had killed their livestock.

A Turkana girl (above) from the western shores of Lake Turkana. The Turkana are pastoralists, but unlike other pastoralist societies, the close proximity of the immense lake has encouraged them to become skilled fishermen. Apart from fishing, the Turkana maintain herds of camels, cattle, sheep and goats. In the harsh environment where this tribe lives, only the higher hills in the west contain grazing suitable for cattle, while sheep and goats are able to survive on the shrubs and bushes.

The Samburu (right) inhabit the region north of the Ewaso Nyiro River. The Samburu are close relatives of the Maasai and carry out a pastoral lifestyle that has been little influenced by the modern age. It is not unusual to encounter a lone Samburu man, dressed in red and carrying nothing besides a spear, wandering across the desert. Although the Samburu people depend largely on their livestock herds for sustenance, in the high-lying country at Maralal crops are also grown.

Nomadic pastoralists (left) water their camels at the Ewaso Nyiro River, Samburu for 'river of brown water'. The river never reaches the sea but disappears into the Lorian swamp, unable to proceed any further across the dry sands of the Sabena Desert. Lined by doum palms, the river meanders through a rugged landscape of inselbergs of volcanic rock dominated by the imposing rock face of the 2 000-metre-high Ol Lolokwe. Three national reserves (Samburu, Buffalo Springs and Shaba) border the river and provide important habitats for the wildlife.

A Rendille woman making pottery (above). As the Rendille tend herds of goats, sheep and camels, they occupy those regions that are too arid for hunter-gatherer groups. They are able to survive in the inhospitable Chalbi Desert, partly by adhering to elaborate customs that govern contentious issues such as water rights and inheritance. In Rendille society, married men, women and young children live in settlements near wells. Acacia branches and sisal mats are used to construct dwellings, and their few luxuries, such as jewellery or cloth, are obtained by barter.

The succulent desert rose (above left) produces delicate white flowers fringed in red even under extremely harsh conditions. The plant grows up to two metres in height and thrives in sandy or rocky woodlands. The sap of the desert rose is poisonous and has been used to coat arrows.

North of Mount Kenya (opposite), the endless vistas, dry acacia woodlands, and rugged outcrops of volcanic rock stretch out to the distant horizon. In this region, George and Joy Adamson carried out their research on the rehabilitation of orphaned lions, leopards and cheetahs.

The beisa oryx (above) of the northern areas closely resembles the gemsbok of southern Africa. Separated by many thousands of kilometres of woodland, the current distribution pattern of oryx suggests that arid regions must at one stage have covered much of Africa. Beisa oryx live in herds of up to 40 animals. They are able to survive for long periods in areas where surface water is absent and depend on vegetation for moisture. In Kenya, the animals south of the Tana River are known as fringe-eared oryx, a subspecies recognized by long black hair tufts on the ears and a richer brown skin colour.

The long-necked gerenuk (left) is an unmistakable gazelle of the dry bushland; and is superbly adapted to arid conditions. The name gerenuk is derived from the Somali language. When feeding, the animal stands on its hind hooves, its long neck extended to reach the higher leaves on bushes beyond the reach of other antelope.

Cheetah (opposite) are still widely distributed in savanna country in Kenya. Despite the country's much publicized rate of human population growth, these vulnerable predators still occur in all the major national parks and reserves. Throughout Africa, cheetah seem to have fared better in semi-arid savannas where human densities remain low.

Elephants (above) in the Samburu National Reserve delight visitors from one of the reserve's game lodges. The elephant is the largest of the land mammals. In order to maintain their enormous bulk, elephants spend most of their time eating and drinking. Individual elephants may consume 150 to 300 kilograms of vegetation in a day and, when it is readily available, are capable of drinking as much as 220 litres of water in the same period of time. In recent years Samburu has become a popular game-viewing destination. The reserve's diversity of game and easy accessibility has encouraged the development of five lodges (including the Samburu Serena Lodge) and luxury tented camps.

Kirk's dik-dik (top) is a small antelope that frequents thickets and low thorn bush, especially in dry regions. Dik-diks are browsers and feed mainly on leaves, although grass shoots are sometimes eaten. In parts of their range, the distribution of Kirk's dik-dik overlaps that of Guenther's dik-dik, recognized by a grey coat, a more pronounced elongated snout, and the absence of a white ring around the eyes.

The Samburu Serena Lodge (above) boasts thatched bandas situated among tall riverine trees on the banks of the Ewaso Nyiro River. The rugged hills of Samburu are home to many leopards. At two of the riverside lodges, Samburu and Samburu Serena, bait is placed out at night to lure leopards. Bones placed on the river bank often attract crocodiles from the river, and these reptiles feed within a few metres of the guests.

About 200 elephants (right) inhabit the Samburu and Buffalo Springs reserves. Elephants are often seen crossing the Ewaso Nyiro River, or feeding along the banks. In the past they were widely distributed throughout Kenya's northern regions, but wide-scale poaching eliminated many herds. Since the Kenya Wildlife Service adopted stringent measures to eliminate poaching, many elephant populations are recovering.

The reticulated giraffe (right) is perhaps the most attractive member of northern Kenya's unique wildlife. This species occurs in the arid savanna country that stretches north of Mount Kenya. Its rich reddish-brown markings and white basal skin colour differ substantially from those of the Masai giraffe. The latter also has only two horns whereas the reticulated has a third on the forehead.

The exquisite Grevy's zebra (opposite top) is the largest of the three zebra species occurring in Africa. Grevy's zebra inhabit semi-arid scrub and grassland, but can survive in desert country if permanent water is available. Apart from a small population that survives in Ethiopia, this species is restricted to Kenya and has been extinct in Somalia since 1973. The Samburu and Buffalo Springs reserves provide an important range for about one-quarter of the national population of 6 000 animals.

The Yellow-necked Spurfowl or Francolin (opposite bottom) is the most common of the 12 species of spurfowl that occur in East Africa. The bird's yellow throat is conspicuous and it is easily separated from similar species. The Yellow-necked Spurfowl frequents dry bush country and woodlands. During early morning and late evening, the loud, grating call of the spurfowl is often heard and assists the bird-watcher in locating these superbly camouflaged birds.

Shaba National Reserve (left) is largely unknown and seldom visited by package tours. It lies to the east of the main road that runs north from Isiolo to Moyale on the Ethiopian border. Shaba covers an area of 239 square kilometres. The name, Shaba, meaning 'copper', stems from a copper-coloured sandstone hill that lies just south of the reserve. The Ewaso Nyiro River flows through an intriguing series of gorges and rapids along the northern boundary of the reserve.

A Ndorobo hunter (bottom) still practises the dying craft of bow and arrow making. Arrow poison is prepared from a variety of sources, in particular the poison berry bush. Ndorobo means 'people without cattle', and the name was given to the group of hunter-gatherers by the Maasai.

The Martial Eagle (below) is Africa's largest eagle – it has a wingspan of over two metres and can weigh up to six kilograms.

Adamson's Falls (above). The muddy waters of the Tana River tumble over the falls on the southeastern boundary of the Meru National Park. The 870-square-kilometre park dates back to 1959 when the local Wameru council took a decision to protect the region's wildlife. Meru is widely regarded as one of the most unspoilt of Kenya's parks. Mount Kenya is often visible in the far distance, and sunsets over the nearby Nyambeni range are frequently spectacular. Rain falling on the hills to the west gives rise to many streams which cross the park before joining the Tana River.

A leopard (right) surveys the surrounding arid savannas from its rocky fortress in northern Kenya. The landscape over much of this region is rocky and rugged – ideal habitat for leopards. These stealthy cats are common in the Samburu National Reserve and are widely distributed over the region where suitable habitat exists, including even the commercial cattle ranches of the Laikipia district. Leopards have been sighted at an altitude of 4 600 metres on Mount Kenya. Joy Adamson's book *Queen of Shaba* described the introduction of the leopard cub, Penny, to the wild.

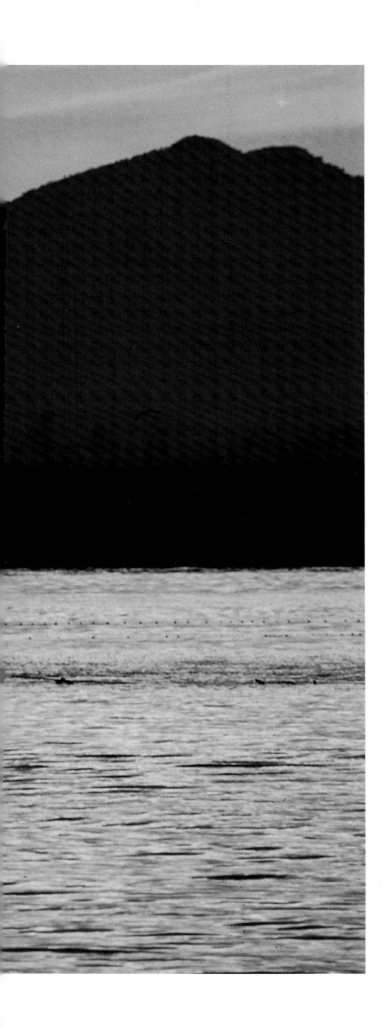

SOURCE OF THE NILE

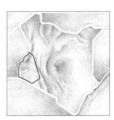

JUST OVER ONE HUNDRED YEARS ago, finding the source of the Nile became an all-consuming passion among learned circles in Victorian England. Two ill-suited explorers, Richard Burton and John Hanning Speke, journeyed inland to search for the river's beginnings. Speke discovered an enormous inland lake covering an area almost the size of Scotland, and named it after Queen Victoria. He assumed that Lake Victoria was the source of the Nile. Subsequent explorations by Stanley confirmed the accuracy of Speke's theories.

Today, the lake is the centre of activity in western Kenya. Kisumu, on the eastern shore of the Winam Gulf, has grown rapidly and is Kenya's third largest town. Connected to Nairobi in 1902 by what has been termed the Lunatic Line, the town serves as both a railway terminal and major port. Cargo is shipped across the lake to ports in Uganda and Tanzania.

Colourful Luo fishing dhows, little changed in their design since the days of the slave trade, ply the lake's waters in search of tilapia and the world's largest freshwater fish, the gigantic Nile perch. On Rusinga Island, the tomb of one of the greatest Luo politicians, Tom Mboya, stands sentry at his home village.

Much of the land in this region lies above 1 500 metres. In this fertile area cash crops such as tea, coffee, sugar, wheat, fruit, and timber sustain one-third of Kenya's people. Kenya's tea industry centres on the town of Kericho. Kenya is the fourth largest producer of tea and sales now comprise about 20 per cent of export earnings.

North of the lake, the imposing summit of Kenya's second highest mountain, Elgon, straddles the Ugandan border. The mountain's lower slopes are blanketed in dense forest and contain a number of caves that have been extensively mined by elephants over the centuries in search of mineral-rich rock.

Luo fishermen (left) bring their catch ashore at Kendu Bay, a town that overlooks the Winam Gulf, Lake Victoria's narrow eastern inlet that averages 20 kilometres in width. The Luo are one of Kenya's largest groups and number about 3.5 million people. It is thought that they migrated south from the Sudan at the end of the fifteenth century.

Fishing nets (left) at a fishing village on the shores of Lake Victoria. The second largest freshwater lake in the world, Lake Victoria occupies an area equal to the state of Sri Lanka. The shallows adjoining the convoluted shoreline and the lake's many islands provide ideal breeding grounds for fish. Lake Victoria's harvest of Nile perch and tilapia greatly exceeds yields from Kenya's coastal waters.

Small fish are laid out to dry (above) on Mfangano Island. The island is densely populated and much of the land is cultivated. In recent years the island has become a popular fishing resort. On nearby Rusinga Island is the tomb of one of Kenya's most talented politicians, Tom Mboya, who was widely tipped as the natural successor to Jomo Kenyatta before he was assassinated in 1969.

Mfangano Island Camp (above) has become a popular retreat for fishermen in recent years. Accommodation consists of six comfortable thatched cottages situated near the lake shore. The camp is renowned for its catches of Nile perch. The largest fish caught on a line (by a fisherman staying at Mfangano) weighed 73 kilograms. Compared to many of the Rift Valley lakes, Lake Victoria is relatively shallow and more productive.

Brightly painted Luo fishing canoes (opposite) line the shore on Mfangano Island. Originally the colours represented wealth, and the more colourful a canoe, the wealthier its owner. Now that paint has become readily available, the canoes no longer have a symbolic value. However, change has by no means diminished the art of canoe making. The Luo construct their own canoes from the wood of the mvule tree.

A 16-kilogram Nile perch (above) caught from a boat off Mfangano Island Camp. Known to the locals as *mbuta*, it is the largest freshwater fish in the world, and was introduced to Lake Victoria from Lake Albert in Uganda. The largest Nile perch recorded weighed over 240 kilograms and was netted at Homa Bay. Since the Nile perch was introduced, catches of the more edible fish species such as tilapia have declined.

Dhows (above) have sailed the waters of Lake Victoria since the time of the slave trade. In design and construction, they have changed little since the days of David Livingstone, the Scottish missionary and explorer who dedicated his life to the halting of the African slave trade in the mid-nineteenth century. After Livingstone's death, the journalist Henry Morton Stanley was sent by two of the most well known London newspapers to settle the controversy surrounding the search for the source of the Nile. Stanley's expedition reached the lake in March 1875. He thoroughly explored the circumference of Lake Victoria by sailing around it for 57 days, and confirmed that only one river flowed out of it.

Known to the Luo as omena (opposite top), the small fish *Engraulicypris argenteus* is similar to a sardine and, once dried, forms an important source of protein for the people bordering several of Africa's Rift Valley lakes. Omena feed on zooplankton in deep water and therefore occupy a niche that is often underutilized in freshwater ecosystems. Lake sardines do not occur in all of the African lakes, and have been successfully introduced into some of the larger areas of water. However, their ecological interaction is not fully understood and current thinking warns against such introductions. At night, fishermen lure these tiny fish to their boats by suspending kerosene lamps above the water of the lake.

The Fish Eagle (right) has a haunting call that is unmistakable and is often referred to as 'the call of Africa'. It frequently perches in trees on the water's edge and, when calling from its perch, throws back its head. Although Fish Eagles have been known to catch waterbirds, they feed mostly on fish. These graceful raptors are common wherever fish can be found.

Mount Elgon National Park (opposite top left) lies on the eastern flank of Mount Elgon, an ancient volcano that rises to 4 322 metres. An enormous mountain, Elgon measures 80 kilometres in diameter at its base. The mountain's lower slopes are clothed in *Podocarpus* forests.

The Giant Kingfisher (opposite top right) is the largest of the African kingfishers. Although this bird is widely distributed throughout East Africa, it is most often encountered along mountain streams bordered by forest. The forests that cover the lower slopes of Mount Elgon provide the Giant Kingfisher with an ideal habitat.

Little Bee-eaters (above) huddle together for warmth in the crisp air of a highland dawn. Little Bee-eaters are often seen in pairs or small groups near rivers or in open woodlands. The birds usually perch on low branches, from which they frequently dart to catch insects on the wing.

Saiwa Swamp (opposite bottom) is Kenya's smallest national park, consisting of a two-square-kilometre refuge for the swamp-dwelling sitatunga. The sitatunga's elongated hooves enable it to live permanently in swamplands. This antelope is largely nocturnal and spends much of the day hidden in papyrus.

Tea plantations (left and right) on the highlands near Kericho – Kenya's 'tea capital'. Conditions for growing tea are ideal and rain falls throughout the year. Kenya is the fourth largest producer of tea, and Kenyan tea usually fetches the second highest price on international markets. The crop now contributes about 20 per cent of Kenya's export earnings. Tea was first grown in the district in the 1920s from plants brought from India and Ceylon. Kericho's Tea Hotel, in the centre of a tea estate, is a popular retreat.

Workers sort coffee beans (above) before they are sent for processing. Arabica coffee is grown on the fertile lower slopes of Mount Elgon. Coffee plants usually begin to bear five years after planting; the berries are then hand-picked and sorted.

The Cherangani Hills (overleaf) form one of the highest elevations in Kenya. These hills plunge from an altitude of 3 300 metres down the Elgeyo Escarpment to the dry floor of the Kerio Valley, a drop of over 1 700 metres.